HISTORY ON THE STAGE

HISTORY ON THE STAGE

Children make plays from historical novels

Edna Conrad & Mary Van Dyke

VNR VAN NOSTRAND REINHOLD COMPANY
NEW YORK CINCINNATI TORONTO LONDON MELBOURNE

ACKNOWLEDGMENTS

To Joseph Barnes, whose experience and wisdom steered us in the right direction.

To E. C. Hamilton and Michael Mahony, photographers, who spent long hours with cameras set, waiting for the right moment, while we fumbled through rehearsals.

To Jon Baugh for costume drawings, which we will continue using as patterns in our playmaking.

To Joi Staton, who deciphered our handwritten manuscript and typed it into readable form.

To Isabelle Suhl, for her help in compiling the list of suggested books at the end of this book—and for her help over the years.

And particularly to Ted Johnson, our editor at Van Nostrand Reinhold, who worked patiently and good-humoredly with us; struggled with us and for us; and by steadfast efforts brought this book to fruition.

Van Nostrand Reinhold Company Regional Offices:
New York Cincinnati Chicago Millbrae Dallas
Van Nostrand Reinhold Company International Offices:
London Toronto Melbourne
Copyright ©1971 by Litton Educational Publishing, Inc.
Library of Congress Catalog Card Number 76-148265

Designed by Jean Callan King
Photographs by E. C. Hamilton and Michael Mahony
Drawings by Jon Baugh
Published by Van Nostrand Reinhold Company, 450 West 33rd Street, New York, N.Y. 10001
Published simultaneously in Canada by Van Nostrand Reinhold Company Ltd.
1 3 5 7 9 11 13 15 16 14 12 10 8 6 4 2

Dedicated to all the 7th and 8th grades
who worked with us on the dramatizations
which started us on this book.

Contents

Preface

Isn't it strange—almost beyond belief, since every human being is born an actor and remains one until his death—that schools make such small use of this very human talent?

Certainly we know that for young children it is their natural way of learning to understand the complexities of the world they are so busily discovering. We call this "play" and tolerate it, or even enjoy and foster it, but still we can hardly wait to start teaching them *our* way.

The truth is that well into the teens, children still "come to life" and learn in depth at a phenomenal pace if we encourage dramatics in the classroom: not the giving of plays written by others, so exciting and dear to thespians of greater age, but the extension into early childhood and adolescence of the earlier play of the very young. All they need is to put what they are learning both in and out of school into dramatic form. Gifted teachers who realize the amazing value of this kind of experience of learning are able to channel history, social studies, sometimes even science and math into dramatic forms.

Alfred North Whitehead, a great teacher, philosopher, and mathematician, said, "True learning comes from firsthand knowledge and is the ultimate basis of the intellectual life," and "To a large extent book learning conveys secondhand information, and as such can *never* rise to the importance of immediate practice."

All forms of acting and re-enacting and playing can be used as an agent for putting together and experiencing knowledge. Yet why is this wonderful opportunity for greater understanding and learning so often ignored, or bound in by so many restrictions that it is stifled and its value all but lost?

Perhaps after you have read this book you will be inspired to try its ideas with your children. I promise you, you will be as excited and deeply satisfied as they are.

It was a lucky weekend for me when, quite by chance, I read Edna Conrad and Mary Van Dyke's manuscript. Here at long last is a book so specific, so aware of the teacher's misgivings, so enthusiastic, so all-inclusive and thorough, so positive in its reiterations of the rewards to be reaped, that it cannot fail. Even the fainthearted should find enough support—if they have the smallest stirrings of sympathy with the dramatic idea—to be able to go ahead and try it.

Here are specific suggestions based on actual successful experiences. It is such a marvelous idea to use historical novels or stories which have caught the fancy of children as a basis for their dramatizations. Please, please try it. The children's reactions cannot fail to carry you along. It can be full, true learning at its very best, and deep and real and memorable—built in forever, one might say.

Jean Murray
Director, City and Country School, New York City
May 1971

9

PROLOGUE:

Why Do It at All?

The most direct way of explaining why we value play projects is to describe our earliest experiences with them.

So far as the school was concerned, what we were doing was getting a play ready for an assembly program. But we wanted a lot more than just a play for assembly. We wanted all the children to be involved in a project that would use as many facets of their learning as possible. Generally, creative drama is isolated from the rest of school work. In fact, in most junior and senior high schools, academic work is isolated from all the arts. What we wanted was a merging of drama and academic work, particularly social studies: a merging of emotion and intellect.

We found that there is a dearth of dramatized social studies material for junior high school children. And so we hit upon the idea of dramatizing a historical novel of a sort that kids this age like to read. The ideal play would be one dealing with the particular period of history they were studying—in this case, American history, from the explorers on. There are excellent plays set in this period, but they are for adult actors and an adult audience. There are also countless plays for children about George Washington, Betsy Ross, Paul Revere, and so on, but while the facts are there, these plays often seem less adult than our students like to consider themselves, or than we consider them.

This was to be a semester-long project in social studies and English, to be brought to life by dramatization and production. If we had the class just learn lines quickly and get up on the stage and recite them, it would be empty and a little embarrassing to think about later. But if the play was made by the students and interwoven with other studies, a permanent pride in learning would come with their wholehearted involvement in creating a play, and furthermore there would be school time available. Charades, or impromptu improvised scenes in the classroom, can be considered dramatizations; but we wanted a production—to be done in front of the whole high school—that children this age could be proud of, and one which would be rewarding enough to justify a long project, somewhat like an extended term paper or a week-long trip planned around the curriculum. So we launched on this program of mutual stimulation. Fortunately, we were in a school that subscribed to this kind of education.

This is a brave concept and in keeping with the best traditions both of education and of the theater. But—let's face it—it's hard work. We found that out, but we found much more. We found that it is a grueling experience and takes much time but that time and trouble are indispensable to achieving the heightened sense of learning that made it worthwhile for the children. The excitement and feeling for their work produced a self-propelled activity on their part that made us go back to this kind of project year after year, in spite of the time and work and confusion.

Almost a year after one of our most successful productions, when we had decided to put some of our ideas about our playmaking into writing, Mary invited some of the children who had been in the production to a Sunday-morning brunch at her apartment, to talk over what they remembered about the play and their work on it. We taped all the talk that morning. It is a jumbled collection of remarks by enthusiastic kids with their mouths full of buns and strawberry jam, happily reminiscing over the last year's play with us, and getting caught up in the excitement of it all over again. What we got on that tape seemed to us an extraordinary expression of their involvement in the project. This spurred us on to complete this book. It really had happened to them; they would always be a little different because of this experience. What we had learned from Winifred Ward and from Hughes Mearns had happened for us. In his book *Creative Power,* Hughes Mearns says, "Just to be—really be—another person in an undistinguished play is to make one immeasurably free forever."

Through these years, we and the children have evolved a way of working, and in this book we have tried to share those ways with you. However, each class and each teacher is so different that your experience may be very unlike ours. That is as it should be, if you are working creatively.

Our most recent play, and the one that the photographs in this book record, was based on Edna Ferber's novel *Show Boat.* We have included at the back of this book the script that our junior high schoolers wrote. When you look at the script, it will look on the page very much like all other plays, good or bad, written for hundreds of years. To appreciate the reach of their work, you should first read the novel from which the students made their script. Read the book, and realize that these youngsters took this novel, and took their history books, and by selection, improvisation, and writing, wove the material into a new form—a play. The play was certainly not good or successful in the way the novel is. But when you read this script, remember yourself at twelve years, and you may be surprised, as we were, at how much they understood, and could turn into acceptable theater. This kind of training awakens them to many qualities in a good professional production. Not that we want them to become professional playwrights, but we do want them to be awakened in all their schoolwork. To extract the most meaningful moments from a man's or a woman's life, and arrange them to hew to the line of your assumed theme, is no mean achievement for junior high school students. It is that process which we cherished and clung to as good education. And the children loved it.

One of our distinguished playwrights, Arthur Miller, once said to a group of our older students, "In writing a novel you get a second chance. You can go back and explain what you meant by having a person say something. In a play, you say it once, and it must stand." In spite of this difficulty, we do subscribe to the notion that dialogue is a vivid way of clarifying ideas, and so it came about quite naturally that we thought of writing out and answering a teacher's probable questions, as a way of explaining the steps of our work process. We don't expect you to take those steps as an inevitable work order. Core projects involve development in many areas simultaneously. And so, neat as we have tried to be, you will find the development of the script mixed in with playing characters, and even with trying on costumes. If you can accept this flow back and forth without feeling that it is too chaotic, then this method is for you.

Of course, there could easily be other questions you could ask, as your circumstances will be different from ours. But it is an integral part of the process that you adapt to your own circumstances; this makes it an exciting and creative experience.

It's happy for the children that we believe that you needn't always sit at a desk to write a play. What is more, you can learn without sitting at a desk. In fact, you probably haven't learned fully until you are not sitting at a desk.

It may seem to you that this book is more about play production than it is about history. Perhaps the children react that way also. That suits us, because we know that hidden away behind every moment of the production is a wealth of research by the children, and information being put into practice. The material of the history courses is there, whether we call it history or a play.

At the end of the book we have put a list of stories and novels which have the two characteristics of being good for social studies content, and in addition have the excitement of plot, personality, and talk that leads to emotional involvement. (Most of them are protected by copyright, and although copyright law is not completely clear on the sort of use we make of historical novels, we advise the teacher to ask the publisher for permission before dramatizing a book.) There are many books not on the list that could be dramatized, and some that have been, but we were interested in finding books with historical content and vital living experience. There are other books on the list that help to give a sense of a period or person. Some of these might be dramatized, but we included them particularly for reading. Scenes can be taken from them effectively without using the whole book. Also in the list are reference books with helpful information for research and play-producing.

Over and above the intellectual exercise of working on a play is the personal growth that comes from learning how to work constructively with a large group for a common goal. In our competitive society there are few opportunities for the flow of give and take in achieving the end we are working for.

At one of our breakfast meetings, John R. said, "We finally got together again. I don't remember how. Some miracles happened."

When a somewhat similar project was being carried out in an older class, one of the girls said, on reporting on the production process, "I think that one of the unique aspects of that two-week period was that at one time or another everyone found himself being ordered around by a fellow classmate who often just didn't have the time to be tactful. There was friction and hostility, actually less than I expected, as we became increasingly tense and tired. Yet, an important part of the closeness that evolved within the class came from a growing respect for the work others were doing.

"Everyone in the class was able to think past himself, and a very tender relationship developed among us; we were careful because we knew everyone was tired, and yet we were still honest. And we began to understand that working together is the only way to work, regardless of college pressure, senior slump, grades, etc.

"...at a time when it might well have been each man for himself, there was great thoughtfulness: people were helping one another wipe off excess makeup; some were doing last-minute mending jobs on others' costumes; girls were fixing each other's hair before they had done their own. These two hours before we gave our first performance showed me how close we had grown, and how much we had forgotten ourselves to work for something that belonged to all of us."

People are beautiful when they concentrate.

STEP ONE:

The Teacher
Chooses the Book

A. WHY NOT LET THE CHILDREN DO IT?

For the most part, you, the adult, must choose the book, as few children have a wide enough reading experience; nor do they know what will make good dramatization. However, if they are deeply involved in a period of history, it is possible that one of them will have read a book on the period, and come up with an excellent suggestion—happily for you. *They* would probably prefer to choose from among several books if you give them a synopsis of the stories, and show them possibilities for staging and costumes. Take a look at section B below, and you will see why choosing is just too much for junior high school students. In our first plays we let the children waste too much time and creative energy getting bogged down at this stage.

Perhaps the difficulties of producing that would come up in any school might discourage you from choosing a particular story. For the production of *Show Boat* we had the difficulty of having less time for the project that we'd ever had; and we had also the problem of staging a boat. But there is almost always a way of working out the difficulties, if the story has tremendous appeal for your group, and has the dramatic qualities that we mention in the next section.

B. WHAT DO YOU HAVE TO LOOK FOR IN A BOOK
TO BE DRAMATIZED?

1. Look for a book that is believable to *your* children. Even if a book is difficult for an average seventh or eighth grader to read, and deals with emotional problems that seem rather mature, or is without much dialogue, it can be used effectively if, in reading aloud, some of the children can recognize the dramatic conflict that is involved.

For example, in the book which inspired our play *Young Jefferson,* there are only a few lines of dialogue telling of the will left by Tom Jefferson's father. However, the will involved the bequeathing of slaves as property, and slavery was a basic theme throughout the whole of Tom Jefferson's life. Our class could readily see the connection between this early experience of his, and his writing of the Declaration of Independence, which became the opening scene of our drama, with flashbacks to episodes in Tom's life. The present black revolution adds heightened interest to this problem of Jefferson's.

This past year our social-studies program covered the post-Civil War period, and we found that there were very few suitable novels to choose from. *Show Boat* turned out to be a very happy choice. It is full of carefully researched information on the racial attitudes and ways of life of a century ago, and one of its main dramatic elements, the constant conflict between Magnolia and her mother, made it instantly appealing to an eighth-grade group. The book does present some difficulties to children—it was written for adults, the plot is intricate, and the style is a reflection of the manners and language of the period. But because it was challenging, it was rewarding too, in ways that a novel written especially for the young cannot be. The children thoroughly believed Edna Ferber's picture of the perennial child-adult conflict, and so they were able to believe in the historical setting too.

2. The book must have the appeal of reality, but not a reality so close to their immediate personal problems as to be embarrassing. One year we tried a book that dealt with modern problems in a school situation, but it was too emotionally exposing for twelve-year-olds. It was asking them to admit to having problems that they self-consciously pretended to be beyond, in order to feel grown-up. The relationships between the characters in the novel were too much like the experiences of our children; and, further, they were embarrassed by the obvious goodness of the hero. On the other hand, *Show Boat* with its Mississippi riverboat setting provided enough distance to play out family relationships comfortably.

Experience in school has taught children that educational movies and history books are often dull. One purpose of dramatizing material from their history class is to make academic learning come alive. So naturally, you choose a lively fiction book about something they are studying, or one that fits in with the year's work. We have suggested some titles at the end of this book, and most teachers will have ideas of their own or will know a librarian who can make recommendations.

In this kind of dramatization the children need factual information as the firm ground on which to build their dramatic action. So, pick a book which is comparatively accurate historically.

The novel on which *Young Jefferson* was based was difficult reading for the

A little worry helped.

Checking out the script.

children, but important American history. We got a picture of Williamsburg life, the function of the House of Burgesses, and particularly the forces leading to the Declaration of Independence, along with a personal story of Thomas Jefferson. These are important historical facts, which we got from a novel instead of from a textbook.

Show Boat, according to Edna Ferber, is neither history nor biography, but fiction. But to write the book she studied the period thoroughly, so it is inevitable that one gets a picture of the period, although facts of "history" are seldom mentioned.

For facts of history, Esther Forbes' novel *Johnny Tremain* is a gem. Johnny is a boy in Boston during the Revolutionary period.

In the drama class the children and teacher had discussed Broadway productions and movies based on history or current events. This prepared the children for accepting material from history for their own dramatization. Some that were discussed were:

The Miracle Worker—	Helen Keller
Paint Your Wagon—	the Gold Rush
Inherit the Wind—	the Scopes trial
All That Money Can Buy—	Daniel Webster in New Hampshire
Fiddler on the Roof—	Scholem Aleichem's Poland
Cabaret—	night club in wartime Berlin
The Heiress—	Washington Square, New York
1776—	the Declaration of Independence

Naturally, you will have to explore the current movies or plays in your area to help you in your discussion. The winter that we wrote up this project saw the opening of the prize play *1776* and the film *The Lion in Winter,* which pleased us by proving how utterly delightful historical facts can be on the stage. Isn't it from plays and novels that we most vividly get a picture of history?

You needn't feel obliged to work out a full three-act play. Sometimes a series of scenes from different books makes a good program, if the scenes have some thought or idea in common. For example, once we improvised and played a series of scenes dramatizing the colonists' defiance of British tyranny. Some were quiet, like Roger Williams slipping away in the night to go to another colony to preach. Some were explosive, like the Boston Tea Party. And some were conniving, like blowing out the lights to seize the Connecticut Charter at Hartford.

3. Don't worry if the book you choose doesn't have exactly the right number of characters, although you mustn't do a play with only one or two if you have a large class. Scenes can be added that are not in the book, if they help the play. One of our projects was based on *Johnny Tremain,* in which at one point the hero, a young boy who has badly burned his hand, is walking along a wharf and thinking despairing thoughts. Since the thoughts were all in Johnny's mind, we staged it as a dream. In order to get this, we had the children improvise what they might think if *their* hands were injured. Then out of their thoughts we made a "stream of consciousness" scene in which the boy wove his way along the street, and voices

from the background said his angry thoughts, and people passing by made comments about him, such as:

"I hate everybody."

"This never would have happened if my mother had lived."

And passersby said:

"I'd take the lad if it weren't for his hand."

"He was a good worker, but I would have nothing to do with him now."

"It happened on the Sabbath. Wasn't it strange that he was working on the Sabbath?"

"I think he deserved what he got."

"The Good Lord willed it."

There were more such comments, and this involved five or six townspeople passing by, apprentice boys who taunted him, and voices backstage.

Sometimes one sentence in a novel, such as, "It was much discussed at parties," can be built into a major scene with many characters—a ballroom scene. Party scenes are a fine way to get everybody involved, and to get lots of girls to wear pretty clothes. They also add life and color to a play. But you have to work hard to get the deportment appropriate to the period, or they look silly.

Thus in *Show Boat*, because the show-boat audiences were often mentioned in the book we staged an audience entrance coming down the aisles of the auditorium, chatting as they came. Up on the stage, watching the melodrama, they had very specific "lines" to shout at the performers in 1870 style. Because of the dockside life, and the wharves in New Orleans, all kinds of scenes could be added. The melodrama performed by the show-boat troupe could be expanded to include entre'acts, elocution, and music.

4. Pick a book that *you* like, or you will find it difficult to spend time on it. This has to be a happy emotional experience for the teacher, or she just can't stand the strain.

To sum up, here are the attractions of a book we and the seventh graders liked particularly, *Johnny Tremain* by Esther Forbes:

(a) It's a captivating story, and even adults love it.

(b) One of its themes is patriotism, and another is "What it means to grow up."

(c) The chief character is a teen-ager.

(d) The emotions involved are understandable to twelve-year-olds.

(e) The scenes fit in with the seventh-grade history (colonial times).

(f) There is excellent dialogue that gives the children an idea of how it can sound, and starts them on writing scenes.

(g) There are many "juicy parts" as well as historical characters.

(h) Costumes can be varied and convey much of the period, and are easy to make out of old clothes one has on hand.

(i) There is only a small amount of scenery necessary.

(j) The book adds a sense of adventure and suspense to historical fact.

(k) Social studies is really full of drama, and this book helps to prove it to children.

She has learned to listen to her partner.

STEP TWO:
Reading the Book Aloud in Class

A. WHY BOTHER TO READ THE BOOK ALOUD?

Reading the story aloud gives everyone more of a sense of immediacy, especially the slow readers. And the sound of the words begins to transform intellectual concepts into the actuality of dramatic experience and talk. This transforming is the most important part of the dramatic work, even though social-studies material takes first place. Therefore we studiously avoid discussion of professional dramatizations of stories we are using. When we have worked out our play, we all get very excited about seeing how it was done on what the youngsters call "the real stage."

Read the whole book aloud before you make the final choice of scenes. To dramatize you must know the basic concept or theme of the total work so that each scene you choose will further the story line you want, or emphasize the theme, or develop the characters and atmosphere. Be sure to get this across to the children from the very first reading. For instance, in the novel about Jefferson mentioned earlier, some children wanted to use a scene in which Tom Jefferson talks to his father. There was a nice feeling between Tom and his father, and there was lively dialogue already written in the book. But, we finally decided not to use it, even though it was dramatic, because when we had read the whole book, we decided to start the play after the father's death. Therefore, this scene didn't fit into the story line. Dropping it kept the play more unified and at a length that we could handle.

Because it was the first chapter in *Show Boat,* and because they enjoyed Magnolia rejecting her mother, the children wanted to include the birth of Kim, when Magnolia refuses to be bossed by Parthy. But as we went along, they saw that it wasn't so important to our play. *Show Boat* is a long story, and it would have been too ambitious to try to dramatize all of it. Some of the students read it all, but we didn't try to go beyond the first twelve chapters in our dramatization. This meant that the set didn't have to be changed, and the play could end with Magnolia's dramatic departure, while her mother shouted, "The show boat will go on."

25

B. WHO READS IT ALOUD?

The reading takes a long time and can be done best by the teacher, or by good readers in the group. Often students from the class hold the attention of the group better than a teacher does. However, when you are reading you can stop to clarify a word that is essential to their understanding, such as "tidewater planters," "pounds sterling," "crucible," "midwife."

With *Show Boat* we tried an experiment that only partly worked. Decorations had to be made for a Christmas assembly, so they sat down with paper, scissors, and scotch tape, and we read aloud while they worked, presumably with their hands only. They did so much fussing with each other, over how the paper cutting was to be done, that it didn't work very well.

Of course we got off on what a midwife was. Most of them couldn't believe that babies were born out of a hospital and without anesthesia. Many of them were sure she was a witch doctor. We could have spent months just getting them to know and understand the way of life of one hundred years ago.

The reading aloud continued the next day. The rest of the group went on putting Christmas decorations together. It worked this time.

The first go at any technique or set-up throws them, but by the second round they settle in a bit. Remember this and don't get discouraged if it doesn't work the first time.

You can stop to note a conflict that will make a good scene. In *Johnny Tremain* the moment when Johnny walks into the Boston *Observer* Office trying to get a job, and meets Rab, can be the turning point in the story, and so you call it to their attention even though it seems a low-key, unimportant event.

You can show a way to add characters, or a place that points up the theme most clearly. As we read *Show Boat* we stopped to talk about riverside crowds, boat sounds, and all the things that happened around the performance of the melodrama.

From the beginning let the children know that you think this will make a good play. As you read aloud, mark in some way the places in the story that the group thinks will make good scenes. Have the children make lists of characters as they appear. Also, they can write the titles of scenes they would like to have included and the pages in the book on which they occur. This is a fine exercise in note taking, and gives them a feeling of already working on their play.

C. WHEN CAN YOU GET TIME TO READ IT TO THE WHOLE GROUP?

The time for reading aloud comes from:

1. drama periods
2. reading periods
3. social studies periods
4. study periods
5. guidance periods

All these areas are enhanced by the heightened interest of the class aroused by the story, and the activity involved in creating a play. While this is not the major reason for choosing a social-studies novel, having social-studies time certainly is one of the advantages. We know reading aloud is ideal, but if it is impossible, assign chapters to individuals or groups, and have them tell the story to the others.

D. WHAT ABOUT YOUNGSTERS WHO READ THE BOOK AHEAD OF THE OTHERS?

Get several copies of the book, and have them available to the group, so that students who are particularly interested can be reading the story at home and thinking about dramatizing it. Reading and rereading will help them get really familiar with the story and the setting, and give them the chance to dig out the dramatic material while you are reading the book for the first time to the others.

You may need to help them to realize that reading and rereading it many times over is the only way to know it well enough to dramatize it. Some of the children who read *Show Boat* through were the ones who had the clearest sense about dramatizing the part that we did.

STEP THREE:

Using the Stage to Get the Script

A. HOW DO YOU CHOOSE WHICH CHILDREN SHOULD DO THE WRITING, AND HOW DO YOU GET THEM STARTED?

This is a very important question. You yourself must be very clear about it and must make it equally clear to the children. In a project like this, *everyone* is responsible for every phase, and although each person eventually has his own responsibility, he must constantly be aware of what other people do, so that the work of every department relates to the total finished production. Sometimes children are afraid to write for fear they will miss out on the final glory of being on stage. Now is the time to make it clear that everyone is involved, and everyone will have a chance to *act.* You will wonder several times before this is over what possessed you to make this promise. But stick to it. You'll be glad you did when it's over. It's sad to see a few children who slaved backstage left out when the applause is going to the actors.

So—as in so much of this project—the writing gets done by numbers of people in several ways. Usually a few who happen to react to a certain episode want to get together and "write the play." By all means let them—warning them that in a stage production, no first writing stays as it is written. Sometimes the whole class can be divided into small groups according to the number of scenes chosen, and each group takes a try at writing a scene. Try to let them work on scenes they fancy, but once they've started, keep the grouping the same so that they can *struggle* with the work—unless, of course, real hostility breaks out.

Lots of seventh- and eighth-grade youngsters are not quite up to this kind of writing work, and to be faced with an assignment of doing it alone would turn them against the whole project. But they love the idea of "working on a committee" and they learn something about how to do the writing just by being in on the activity.

We scatter around the auditorium, a teacher to each group, to get some writing done, while others work on costumes.

If they have been exposed to "creative dramatics" before you start this play, now is the time to remind them that that is a good way to work on their writing. If they have not had anything like that, let them just write on their own, and bring in improvisation a little later.

These first writings are the beginning of an extraordinary process, which should truly be the heading for this section; "bouncing back and forth from page to stage." As soon as a group has even a little bit written, let them read it aloud on the stage, or in front of the class, pushing furniture aside, so that if they suddenly want to, they can move around. The problem of having enough readable scripts, even for the first few lines, is one of the frustrating experiences that shortens

tempers, and often needs a teacher's help. So, if they are willing, it is sometimes better just to let them *tell* the chain of events. For example:

"The house slaves set out the chairs for the reading of the will, talking about it as they go along. Then Tom's mother comes in. Then Tom's sister. In the meantime other slaves are creeping up to listen outside the window."

The chain of events provides a spine for the scene.

The discussion following this first try, no matter how it is presented, requires the leadership of someone aware of the need to look for dramatic conflict. Dramatic conflict happens when two people or two groups of people want opposite things. It can be pleasant, unpleasant, funny, or tragic. This is the basis for all theater. You don't have to be a theater person, but you must stop being the traditional classroom teacher who needs a classroom and children in fixed rows of desks. You must think in terms of human desires and conflicts.

As soon as a group has read or "told" a scene, everyone has ideas, suggestions, criticisms. Your job will sometimes become that of traffic manager, but that's good because they soon discover how to take stimulation from each other. This first group can now start walking around saying what each one thinks the character he is being *would* say and do, or they can retreat to a corner of the room to write about what they've got from reading or from group discussion, letting the next group present what they have thought out *so far*. Never let them think that they have a finished product at this first try. And for several meetings, start by saying, "Which group has added something, and would like to try it out on the stage?" Or, "Would some group like to try a scene, and walk around on stage just using whatever lines come to you and add whatever seems right?" Now, this may begin to look as if these people might play those parts—and it may turn out that way because they know more about the particular situation than the rest of the class. But try not to worry about that now. And don't let the kids push you into it.

This process of writing, improvising, reading, listening to suggestions, and then rewriting must go on until you have a play that tells a story, has good clear characters, is true to its historical period, and has a clear overall statement or theme. In general, youngsters write skeletons of scenes and you will constantly have to

It takes a long time to think how to end it.

help them put flesh on their ideas—the improvisation helps again. Seldom will they write too much, but either way *you* must keep in mind a play—one that can hold interest. A short vivid production is better than a rambling one. The children may not think of it, but you must remember to keep adding scenes or characters until everyone has a part. This won't happen until fairly late in the process. But don't panic. Your play will be better than one with a neat overorganized plot that the children have had no hand in writing and perhaps don't understand.

During the work on *Show Boat*, we got the children started off by letting them choose a scene that interested *them*. One we called "Out Riding with a Murderer" pleased them although it was in the middle of the play. It was easy to get started with it because the dialogue was in the book, and it had an uproarious "Western" quality, a good deal of humor, and the girls yearned to play Parthy, who is a noisy, forthright character. It gave us all a lift and a good start.

31

B. YOU CAN'T USE THE WHOLE BOOK.
HOW DO YOU SELECT SCENES?

Of course you can't use all of a novel or even all of a short story. The problem usually becomes: What can we afford to cut and still keep the story (1) interesting and (2) dramatic? In the case of *Show Boat* we could cut the plot in half and still have the interesting and dramatic Mississippi River story. The incidental scene of the farm woman bringing jelly to Parthenia which we liked so much could be dropped when rehearsals became too hectic. It's still a nice scene, and it's still in the script.

Some choice of scene is made when the story is being read aloud. Most of them have to be decided on toward the end of the reading, however, for a decision must be made by the group first as to what the theme is. The theme then determines the choice of scenes. In deciding the theme, you must clarify for them the difference between "theme" and "plot." "Plot" is the series of events that lead to a climax and makes a story, whereas "theme" is the overall statement of philosophy or significance that the plot demonstrates.

And they must learn also that a good scene will forward the plot, and/or develop a character, and/or create the atmosphere of the historic period, and still always sound like real people talking. Keep in scenes that will keep the plot or line of events clear. Also keep the scenes that are exciting or dramatic. We included Patrick Henry's "Liberty or death" speech in *Young Jefferson;* it is not necessary to the plot, but it is stirring to the audience, and the kids relish the flamboyance. And in *Show Boat,* it was both exciting and useful to show the kind of melodramatic plays that were acted on the river boat.

Remember to use or concoct scenes with lots of people, or scenes which build the flavor. Kitchen, tavern, or jail scenes, for instance, are excellent for colonial plays. A ballroom scene and a House of Burgesses scene in *Young Jefferson* were concocted to use people. Another example was in *The Devil and Daniel Webster* in which we made a scene in Jabez Stone's kitchen with the whole family desperate over their poverty. It's easy to have all kinds of people all through *Show Boat*—dock workers, audiences, townspeople.

You, the teacher, as well as the children must stay ready to accept a complete rearrangement, if it works into a better play. We decided to use the very end of a book as the opening scene of our *Young Jefferson,* after we had read the whole book and written many of the scenes. In discussion, we decided that the Declaration was the high point of Jefferson's whole life. And since the Declaration of Independence is the essence of American history, it made an excellent thematic opening.

C. HOW DO YOU TEACH THEM TO WRITE DIALOGUE?

Starting to write dialogue is so difficult, and so threatening, that if it's just "made up" by the children, it turns out stilted or is imitative of television. So you *can* make a start by taking some dialogue directly from dialogue in the book. Then, when your novice playwrights get the flavor of it, they can elaborate and give other characters lines in the same style.

Our student adviser comes in with a message but stays, captivated. The theater always gets 'em.

Or you can set up the situation and have them do an actors' improvisation, while part of the group sits watching and takes down dialogue that they think is particularly good.

When we got to the pilot-house scene in *Show Boat*, there were only scattered references to the pilot house through various chapters, and none of us seemed to know quite what to write. Someone got the idea of having the actors up in the balcony over the stage for the pilot house. They loved the idea, even though some of them wanted the whole stage to look like a boat. We made a note that we must get them to a theater, or at least get pictures of stage sets, to show them that naturalism is not the only way to set a stage. When they got up there away from us, they seemed much freer to play at piloting a boat, and such lines as "More steam!" just happened. Even with this improvisational freedom the following dialogue is all that got written for a first draft.

BRIDGE SCENE (MAGNOLIA, ANDY, PILOT)

MAGGIE:	I don't mean. You know that's not what I mean.
PILOT:	During flooding time it's covered up, but during low tide it comes up.
MAGGIE:	Was it there last year?
ANDY:	Where's your mother?
MAGGIE:	Don't ask.
PARTHENIA:	Maggie Hawks, I'll give you to the count of ten to get down here for your arithmetic lesson.
MAGGIE:	I don't wanna do any arithmetic. Why is the river that color?
PILOT:	See that island? It's called Ocean Island.
MAGGIE:	Can I steer the boat?
PARTHENIA:	Is Maggie up there, because—

Just three children standing at the balcony rail—but they are developing what will be the pilot-house scene in *Show Boat*.

It took more improvisation, and discussion, and people who could take random dialogue and weave it into a complete scene to make the script we finally used. A good free improvisation is often better than most writers can dream up.

One day in class when a little girl was playing the clerk and owner of a bakery shop, we suggested that instead of just waiting on the customer, she might be a bit chatty, because later she had to tell this same customer about a strange man who came in every Christmas. Well, during the scene she launched into a story about how she and her sister had inherited the shop when her father died, adding names, dates, and personal data that were hilarious, charming, and added considerably to the story from which the play was taken.

Most children hesitate to do anything like this because it isn't the customary school pattern, but once they see that it is approved, some of them will try and others will eventually join in. It was particularly difficult for the boys in *Show Boat* to let go for the 1860 melodrama, but once one of the boys broke the ice, they all let go with gusto. Maybe overacting freed them to both write and act.

The questions you can keep asking, or having them ask themselves, are:

(a) Does it seem like *that* person talking?
(b) Does it move the story along, or is it "just talk"?
(c) Does it sound like the time in which the story happens? ("OK" just won't do for 1770 in Boston.)
Usually results are better if you let them begin by improvising in their own language, because the most important thing is the dynamics of conflict between people and forces. Then, when they write the dialogue, they can add the flavor of the time.

The children saw that there was a dramatic incident in Peter Jefferson's will leaving slaves as property. However, what they wrote started with the lawyer opening his mouth to read the will. When the will was read, the scene was over. This appeared to be the action of the scene, but there was much more implied in the book, and much more that *they could add.*

We talked about the abruptness of starting with reading the will, and began improvising, getting the room set for a large family gathering. Then we moved

The kids are a marvelous audience for each other, and sit, fascinated, as those on the stage improvise—so that they often forget to write down the wonderful lines that they hadn't thought of before.

"Oh, that's great."

into the children's moods about this situation. One girl came up with these lines, which were just right for the moment: "It's so lovely out, Mother. This is the kind of day Father would have loved to go hunting."

One child remembered that in the book the lawyer was offered refreshments, and this made a nice moment in the scene. The whole pattern of appropriate social amenities had to be developed. This meant that the children had to be helped with proper forms of address and suitable topics of conversation for persons of that class and period.

Then the reading of the will was simple.

Next we had to prepare for the climax of the scene by having the slaves listening outside the window to find out what was going to happen to them. So when Tom left the room and went outside, the scene was set for one of the most important moments in the play, when one of the slaves asks if any of them are to be sold. The question could be taken from the book, but then the book went on to explain Tom's reaction. To make this reaction suitable for the stage, we changed it from descriptive statement to dialogue by having Tom unburden himself to his sister. By now the children playing Tom and his sister were very much involved and could talk back and forth easily to each other on this subject of slavery. They improvised several times, and this is what finally got written down:

TOM: Jane, why do we have slaves?

JANE: I don't know. I suppose it's because Father had them.

TOM: But it's wrong to own anyone. Slaves are human, too.

JANE: I suppose you're right. I have never thought of that. You own Tawney. Why don't you set him free? What about all those other slaves father left you? You could free them, if you want.

TOM: Yes, I could, but—wait, what would they do for a living? No one would hire them. And, anyway, we would go bankrupt if I had to pay for Labor. We're better off this way, and so are the slaves. But still, it's wrong to own another human being. I want to do something about it. But what?

JANE: I don't know, Tom, and neither do you, but when you do, I'm sure you'll do it.

Although many of the ideas in this scene were inspired by the book, as thoughts or statements by the author, the children shuffled them around to make dramatic scenes, with people speaking their thoughts. The creation of this scene was more of an accomplishment than most because in the novel's brief description the intensity was there, but there was no dialogue.

Show Boat was full of dialogue. Edna Ferber is a dramatic writer. But we had to work it into our own play.

We had met in small groups, written on scraps of paper, and improvised over and over. Finally we gathered it all together in fairly readable shape, and got it typed and duplicated. We passed out the collated script, and there was utter silence. Everybody was reading intently, leafing back and forth. Then you could see little smiles, and hear comments like: "I wrote that," or "Gee, this is long," or "Let's publish it." They were terribly proud.

D. WHAT IS MEANT BY "IMPROVISATION" AT THIS POINT?

A great deal has been said and written recently about improvisation as a technique for training and stimulating actors. It is a very old practice; it dates back to Roman comedy, it was essential to the 14th-century commedia dell'arte of Italy, and there was an improvisational theater during the French Renaissance.

Actually it is a "game" deeply rooted in children's play, and therefore it is very usable for your purposes. Children have forever played out being somebody else, or being themselves in another situation. This is exactly what you can get them to do with any situation they can emotionally understand. An essential difference between this approach and the imitative or pantomime approach is that to improvise you must work from *your own feelings or knowledge* and not copy someone else's physical behavior.

Most children don't know what the term "improvisation" means, and it's just as well. It leaves them free to "play it out" without trying to copy grown-ups. Sometimes we have said, "Well, this is the situation—now just do whatever you would do in these circumstances."

Not all children are free enough to improvise on a situation at the beginning, because they don't quite believe that it's really "being in a play," and some will use the freedom of the session to kid around or depart from the situation. But do it half a dozen times using different people. Tell them that in an improvisation there are no "lines" as such. And that out of what everybody does, the writing group for this scene will *gather* the dialogue. Often kids will sit there and write whole scenes as they watch.

Liz was writing a scene for a play in which the hero is being sent from the American colonies to a school in London in 1774. The first writing was this:

> DAN: I have to go to London to school.
> TIM: Why?
> DAN: My father says so.

Obviously, this wasn't enough for a scene. If we said "Write more!" she'd be lost. So, we said, "What would *you* do if your father sent you away to a school you didn't want to go to?" We talked about it, and several children said what they'd do. Then Liz played out this situation on her own. Then we said, "Let's set up a scene like that with Tim, his wife, and Dan." As she began to act Dan, a good-sized temper had developed, but Tim and his wife just stood there. Then we talked again, this time about how we all react to bad news. And we asked, "Would you always tell about it the minute you come in—even to a friend?" Her answer was, "Sometimes I just come in and sit down and don't speak." "Good. Let's try that, and then Timothy is bound to have to ask you why you are so silent." This started the boy playing Timothy watching and listening to Dan, and a scene began to emerge. Tim's wife needed help finding something to be doing while she was listening, because in 1774 poor women seldom sat around doing nothing. Here a whole discussion came up about what women had to do in the house in those days, ending in a search by the children for pictures of dishes and tools of the period, so that costumes and properties entered into the planning. Tim's wife found that folding sheets was something she might be doing. This was a particularly good choice because before Dan came in, she could ask for Tim's help. This may seem chaotic, but eventually it is enthusiastic, and finally even the shy ones want to get up and try it, even if they only repeat what other people have already done and said.

E. WHAT ABOUT MUSIC?

Long before you begin putting the project on the stage, talk with the music teacher, and think about music and how you can use it. Have children search for music of the period. Try to involve children who play instruments. Use music as movies use it—for mood background.

It's a nice project for some child who's interested in music to go to the library to find out who the composers were for that period. A particularly valuable book for finding composers and dances as well as costumes is *Playing Period Plays* by Lyn Oxenford (Coach House Press, 55 West Jackson Boulevard, Chicago, Illinois).

Find a record catalogue. Almost every school has a record player, and records are so good now you can easily find one for background music.

Church music was important in colonial times. Marches and popular songs were made up in all war periods. Each period had its characteristic instruments for sacred or secular music. A study of this can become an interesting project for children with musical interests.

Especially gifted children may like to write their own music for a particular interlude or scene. One group wrote a song of loneliness and anger to be sung in the background as Johnny Tremain wandered along the docks, cursing his fate.

It's worth making an effort to incorporate music because it lifts the play out of *plain* reality, and gives color and imagination to the whole thing, and the audience always enjoys it. *Show Boat* provided a beautiful opportunity because Negro spirituals were what made Magnolia famous in the night clubs of Chicago—songs she had learned from the Negro workers on the Mississippi River boats. The sentimental songs of the period made up the musical entre'act and the concerts given after the play. For the advertising of the Cotton Blossom performances we used a recording of a circus calliope, a trumpet, and a drum. It would have been a good project for some student to tape dock and riverside sounds, but we didn't.

When working in American historical periods, one of the easy ways to get music for these plays is to use folk material.

F. WHAT ABOUT ART?

Art is a subject that lends itself beautifully to stage production. A period of history is identifiable by its physical appearances. So if you have an art teacher who is interested in the history of art, you have an opportunity to work out a successful area of core teaching.

The girls start working on songs of the period.

One of the girls who was not in the main part of the play, and had a lovely voice, sang a Negro spiritual of the period, and acted as narrator for the melodrama in *Show Boat*.

The study of art must include a study of the culture from which it springs. And conversely, the study of history is incomplete without some knowledge of the art of the given period.

The art teacher can be a great help in going into styles of clothing, and color and fabrics. This is also true for furniture. Art, fashions, and history all merge.

Even the use of certain colors typifies periods—Williamsburg blue, traditional white woodwork for the Federal period, and rich, dark colors in Victorian times.

Straight lines dominate early colonial houses and furniture. The Victorians fancied the oval, and late Victorians went wild with curlicues and "gingerbread."

If there is a home economics or sewing teacher, the art teacher and the sewing teacher can join in teaching some of the needle crafts, which are now again popular. For the colonial period the story of the evolution from tapestry to crewel work is fascinating.

Once when we were doing a colonial story, two girls experimented with the colonial techniques of dyeing fabrics with roots and berries.

Most of the practicalities of staging require the working together of all departments, but the making of program covers takes the children directly to the art department. Even if your school has no art department, the classroom teacher can work out interesting art projects connected with the time and place of the play.

G. HOW DO YOU MAINTAIN CLASSROOM ORDER DURING THIS PROCESS?

Don't try to maintain classroom order. There will be the discipline of people pushing ahead toward something they very much want to do instead of traditional classroom order. This is the time when the class cuts loose, and all kinds of things happen. It is a time when scenes are fabricated; when large numbers of characters are added; when some scenes get completely changed from the original concept; when the children get a new appreciation of each other even as they quarrel over which is the "right" way to do things, and turn to texts and reference books with awakened interest; when they struggle with English to make it convey ideas and feelings, and the play form reveals its limits and complexities and opportunities. This whole period of creation is the first thing the children talked about at a breakfast meeting when we asked them what they remembered.

When the children get strongly motivated, they can work well on their own in small groups, in or out of school. Let groups work all over the room at all kinds of preparation, even if it creates a mild pandemonium. It's better than sitting still feeling unnecessary. But don't let the drifters move from group to group. Also, watch for subtle signs of aroused interest in children who seem diffident and only murmur suggestions. Their ideas may be wonderful for the play, and it may be the beginning of a feeling of appreciation and participation needed by a shy child.

Eventually, they all get caught up in the needs of the play. This produces a willingness to subordinate their old habits for the sake of the success of the group project. This is discipline.

Sometimes when we look backstage, we wonder what educator it was who said, "Learning is untidy." We'd like to shake his hand.

STEP FOUR:
Choosing Children for Parts

A. WHEN DO YOU DO THE FINAL CASTING?

Abandon the pattern of "write the whole thing, cast the whole thing, rehearse the whole thing." Casting doesn't happen at a set moment, and yet does get done. Before any parts are definitely assigned to any child, all the scenes are worked over, improvised on, read and reread on the stage. By having scenes read again and again with different children, many surprising abilities show up. When their attention is on the play and not on "trying out for a part," they work more freely and imaginatively.

In the teacher's mind the casting is done fairly continuously, and some parts are even settled with the children. But all along let the children in on why you make certain decisions. Let them see that you are looking for the sharpest portrayal of certain characteristics.

Don't set up a system of casting by having the children vote for each other, because voting too easily degenerates into a popularity contest. Everybody will be happier if the teacher keeps this important responsibility. Even near the end

Some of the students design programs in the art room.

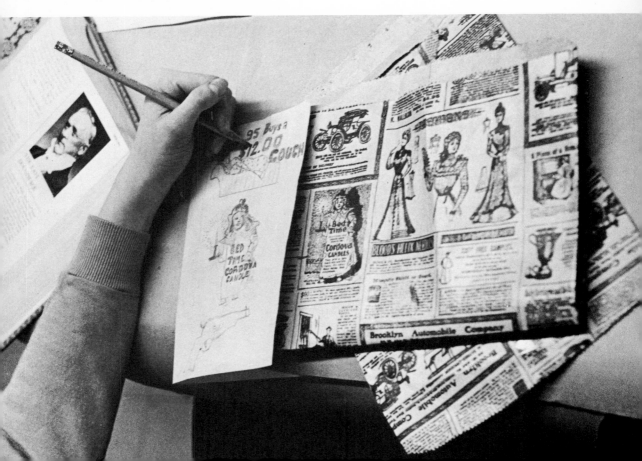

The boys slave over the big sign for the show boat—THE COTTON BLOSSOM FLOATING PALACE THEATER.

These two girls begin to improvise a scene...

we have had to exercise our judgment, and had to change the casting a little. This is possible if the parts changed have not too much to say.

In *Show Boat*, a boy who had not seemed very much interested, and could never be heard during early rehearsals, turned out to be someone always accurate and dependable, and what is known in the theater as a "quick study." So, the day before the assembly, we suddenly gave him the part of Frank in one scene. He had come alive during rehearsals, and could carry more work.

As you cast, remember that each child must appear on the stage; that you must have strong people to carry the play; and that it's your sacred duty to "bring out" certain children. Do the final casting when you see the play taking shape. Assigning parts takes much deliberation. These are not "professional" performances, and the growth of each child is as important as the success of the play. But the play must come off well so that all the children feel good about themselves.

In *Show Boat* Ann demurred rather desperately when she thought we were about to give someone else a part that she had improvised. (She played the part.)

But most of us have large classes and small casts. It may astonish you as a theatergoer that a character with many lines can be played by a different child in every scene, even though this is not customary. In *Young Jefferson*, the chief character, Tom Jefferson, was played by a different boy in each scene. We admit there is a risk of confusing the audience a bit, but one way to keep the character identified is a quick change backstage of a recognizable coat, or some other striking clothing, such as a bright scarf—which means you'd better cast boys of about the same size for one character.

Of course, if you have the time, it helps to have a program mimeographed for the audience, so they can quickly see who's who. The children love making and decorating covers for programs in the art room.

It was clear from the first exercises preparing for the melodrama in *Show Boat* that Mady would play the heroine—she's so very blond, she was so free in taking on the style, and she has such good stage presence. Everyone accepted it with good grace, even though it was a "plum of a part."

If you are one of those fortunate teachers who have a small class, say ten or twelve, you may have to have one child play two or more parts. In *Show Boat*, to give everybody a chance to play some part he particularly wanted, we cast each scene separately with no thought of keeping one person in one part. We all thought Steve was wonderful as Captain Andy; but he was determined to play the drunk in the meoldrama, and we needed him to play Julie's husband in the miscegenation scene. There was some really wild costume changing behind scenes to get him on in all these parts. The white trousers for Captain Andy got passed around backstage. And all the girls who played Parthy managed to have black silk skirts on.

B. HOW CAN YOU TELL WHICH CHILDREN WILL BE GOOD IN A PART?

You can't be sure to cast "perfectly"; individuals will become different during rehearsals. But, as we said before, cast enough strong people to carry the play along, so they can all get a feeling of success.

...and try it over and over...

After the first improvisation between Ila and Emily for the final scene in *Show Boat*, we knew we needed Ila to finish the play to give it the strength it had to have. Because Emily has always been a gentle, quiet girl, we weren't absolutely sure that she would rise to fight Ila. But they worked wonderfully together, and whenever they rehearsed, people stopped to listen. Then one day Emily let go with a genuine emotional explosion that surprised us all. After the assembly program, Emily's big brother said, "I was so surprised. I didn't think she could do anything like that, because I've never heard her lose her temper."

...until finally a scene develops.

Not until the play was over, and we happened to look at the script, did we realize how much this deeply involved little girl had added. The script read simply, "Well, the show boat is going on!" But she had shouted, "I don't need you! The show boat is going on! The *Cotton Blossom* is going on!" Even the most casual kids caught the vigor of her feelings, and clustered around her afterward to share in that success.

Others who are fearful should be put in situations where they don't have to stretch themselves *too much,* so cast them in small parts. With the children you are not clear about, take chances. The play doesn't need outstanding talent, because everyone is to understand everything that's going on and be so steeped in the background that each one participates in every moment and is involved emotionally. Settle for an honest, earnest understanding, and don't aim for that overdrawn projection of character that is often considered "good acting." Study all your children on and off stage.

I want to play Magnolia.

C. WHEN SEVERAL CHILDREN WANT TO PLAY A PART, WHAT DO YOU DO?

Children often find a character, in this process of working out scenes, that they very much want to play. Finding a "small" but picturesque character that the child feels he understands helps to eliminate the problem of too many wanting to "play the lead."

Some children seem never to want anything. When one of these falls in love with a part, *let him have it.*

Some children think they want everything, but what they really want is the biggest part. You have to help these children accept a compromise, by pointing out to them what is important in the parts they have been given. This last problem is not so common in the junior high school, perhaps because they are aware of the importance of each part that adds up to the whole in a play they have written themselves.

It does not mean that everyone will be happy at first. If the play as a project is stressed enough, some of the competitive feelings will become less sharp. Children who are disappointed in their assigned roles will be caught up in the enthusiasm of the play. We don't know whether it was love for the character part, or enthusiasm for the project, but in *Show Boat*, some boys didn't seem to want to get up on the stage at all at first, but these very same boys, as we came to the final performance, were doing enormously responsible work, sometimes even taking more than one part.

At a breakfast meeting with the seventh grade, in two hours of discussion, no one brought up the subject of competition in casting.

STEP FIVE:

Directing & Producing

A. HOW DO YOU GET A CHARACTERIZATION FROM A CHILD ONCE THE PARTS ARE ASSIGNED?

All the work of reading, writing, and arguing has brought them close to the characters—even to the villain, which some customarily docile soul will get great release from playing. Part of the problem of full characterization is solved by your watching from the beginning to see which children have a genuine affinity for a character. In *Show Boat* after Steve did the drunk in rehearsal, no one even tried to play it. It was his. The devotion and extra work that Markle gave to writing the New Orleans dockside scene with Ravenal made us think that he wanted to play a part in that scene. It seemed good to put him in a position of authority, so we gave him the part of the cop.

Sometimes the quietest child has such a yen to be noisy that he plays a noisy part beautifully without much help from you. In one play, Ronnie, who was rather withdrawn, needed very little coaching for the part of a jailor, once he realized that he was supposed to be an ugly, noisy man.

Understanding the *whole* person being played—the many facets of his character—is more important than just saying lines. Get the child to find how his character would walk, move hands, listen; and get him to think about his manner of speech, especially. In *Show Boat* every girl in the eighth-grade group enjoyed striding about like domineering Parthenia Hawks; and all the boys took a try at clawing their whiskers in Andy Hawks style.

Also go back to what we said on improvisation. That is one way of getting into a character. Sometimes it is better for you to work alone with a child, so that he does not have quite so much need to appear successful while trying. Then you can get him to remember some experience or emotion that will let him feel a little like what the character was feeling. In the first scene of *Show Boat*, Alison didn't have to remember very far back to understand "trying to find an arithmetic answer" when her mind wasn't really on it. It was harder for Julie in the miscegenation scene, but finally she found how to feel, as she said, "very scared at being caught."

52

Try the role...

...improvise, revise.

Once a group of three was working on a scene from a story in which some white children were trying to teach their little slave to speak English. Our approach was to suggest that they remember how they had tried teaching their own baby brothers or cousins new words. We talked about this until they were quite back in the spirit of that event. Then we said, "Just do the same thing with Phyllis." It worked.

Another device is to have each child write a letter as if he were the character he is playing, using the language and ideas of the time and place. For example, when we were preparing *Young Jefferson*, we had all the girls write letters—to be sent by messenger, of course—inviting outstanding persons to an evening of music during the "Public Days" in colonial Williamsburg. When we were preparing for *Johnny Tremain*, the boys carried on a correspondence between Mr. Hancock and the merchant, Mr. Light, and wrote articles for the *Boston Observer*, the chief newspaper of the day. Part of the preparation for *Show Boat* was an English assignment to write a character sketch of one of the characters. One young girl started out by writing the following paragraph, and eventually played the part very well.

"Parthy Ann is a very stern, pushy woman who is set on always getting her way. When she notices something she disapproves of she will immediately run to do something about it. If she has an opinion, it is almost impossible to change her mind. Parthy also has much dignity, and when she walks she holds her chin up high. Parthy also will use people in order to make a point or to get a mission accomplished."

In the same way, struggling with costumes and with scenery helps each child to grow in his part, because by immersing himself in the ways of the period, he deepens his performance. Probably this is the real reason for this kind of approach to social studies. Living a historical event stays in your memory longer than just reading about it.

Not all children will achieve effective identification and projection in performance, but every one will grow in some direction.

B. HOW CAN YOU GET EVERY CHILD INVOLVED?

Some children are afraid of a creative experience, because they fear exposing their emotions and betraying their inadequacies. Give them a chance and a nudge, and if they seem adamant about "public" performance, let them operate in a mechanical activity close to where the action is. They'll get used to being active in the group, and after a while they will forget themselves and may want to get on the stage. All children can function better than they usually do.

With the timid child or the shy, quiet one, one must play it by ear, rather than arbitrarily forcing a "contribution from each one." But keep a weather eye out for those who just sit still. They often need help in making the first move toward joining in. It was probably the rehearsals of the 1860 melodrama for *Show Boat* that lured almost the whole class in. After being quite adamant that she *didn't* want to be involved, Debbie couldn't resist. We didn't have her participate immediately, but toward the end she pleaded. Once in, she prompted the entire performance, was responsible for sound cues, and rigged her own backstage prompting light.

Some of our nicest help came from several boys and girls who were not in the group. They came in and helped with sewing and set building, or did small parts, and added to the good tone by their willingness and enthusiasm. By just sitting in the auditorium being interested, they gave the actors a lift. Some of the boys got interested in seeing what was being built in the shop, came to help put the set together, and became very good stagehands.

For some, improvising is too exposing, and so for them nothing happens until there is some physical job to be done, like moving the lights. From such jobs, this boy progressed to setting lights for every scene, and playing two parts as well.

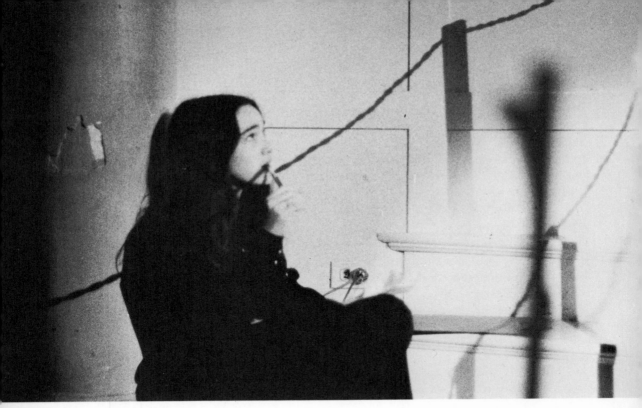

Debbie prompting.

One time we had an unpleasant little girl who at the beginning had seemed ready and willing to sabotage the entire project. There didn't seem to be a big place for her in acting, partly because of her surly manner. We pushed her into so much activity—running for supplies, getting props, making things in the art room, moving furniture—and she put so much of herself into these activities that she became a significant part of the production, and finally lost her surly manner with us.

To find your creative place in a social situation is one of the happiest moments of your life. A boy who had gone through elementary school feeling, and being, only on the edge of things, seemed to fit the part of Jabez Stone in *The Devil and Daniel Webster,* and played it. And from that time on he felt himself more a part of the class, and as a result the class accepted him as one who now belonged.

Some children who are downright disruptive in routine classes respond to this kind of project and become "good citizens." These are the children who have more physical and mental energy than they can use up through ordinary channels. A play done this way challenges them to special effort—in order that the play succeed—and the great variety of demands made on them gives them a feeling of importance.

However, in such a free situation, there are certain children, sometimes more aggressive than able, who want to take over the entire project. Watch these too. Use them, but don't let them dominate to the point of taking all the limelight and thus discouraging the others. Here is the place where the academic whiz kid or the playground bully may have to concede to a limp little fellow who knows just how to play the devil in *The Devil and Daniel Webster.*

It was a good sign of the growing *esprit de corps* when kids who weren't even in the drama group offered to come in during vacation week to help with costumes. Two girls valiantly sewed and pressed, and were part of us.

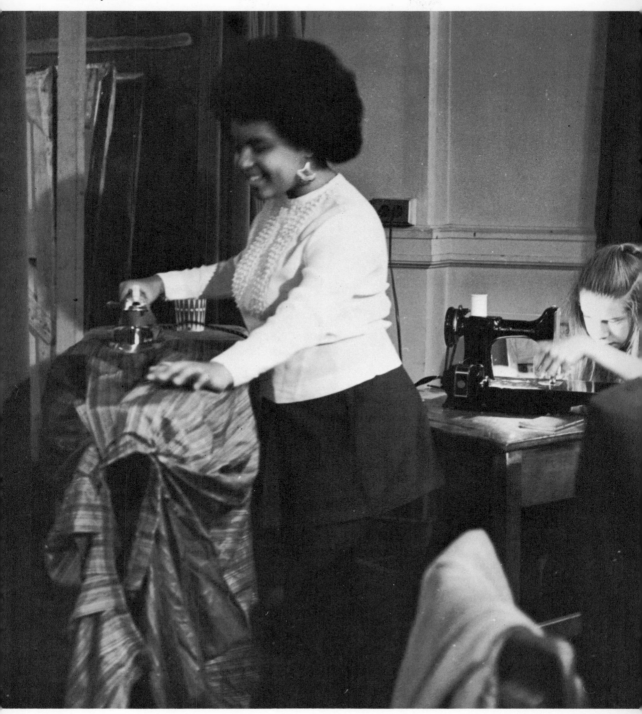

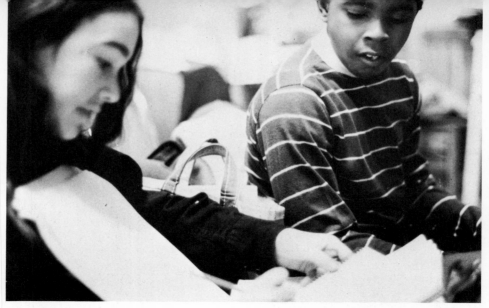

Working out light cues.

C. WHAT IS DIFFERENT NOW THAT YOU ARE "JUST REHEARSING"?

Until the last few run-throughs, there will be constant changes. But there must come a time when emphasis is more on exits and entrances, lights and cues, sound effects, and technical stage details, than on the creative aspects of the script. This was the moment in *Show Boat* when Debbie became indispensable, because she was the only one who was not on stage at all and could "hold book" right through the rehearsal, and she worked with Nat on light cues.

However, just as soon as you make a decision that something is set, someone will come up with an idea—a good one—to change the whole direction of a scene or even the play. You have to know when it's just too late, and you have to say, "No, we had better leave it alone now."

During a rehearsal of *Young Jefferson*, the boy playing Patrick Henry was so stirring in his "Liberty or Death" speech that the class burst into applause, and right then and there they wanted to turn it into a Patrick Henry play. One of our most productive discussions followed. In this discussion we realized that Patrick Henry was a tremendously colorful person, and "Liberty or Death" a perennial theme. But we had decided on the theme of the Declaration of Independence, and had put hours and hours of research and writing into it. Taking Patrick Henry as our subject would mean dropping this story and taking another. Even the children saw that this would be too much. But a year later at that play's breakfast meeting, the youngsters were still keenly aware of how entranced they had been with Patrick Henry.

Don't be afraid that you will destroy creativity by saying, "No, we can't change." If the children have worked out the play to this point, they usually are devoted to the "good of the play," and they are proud of the scenes they have written. They need to learn that creation must be brought to a conclusion. This is one of the great advantages of having a performance as a focal point. Too long-drawn-out a process vaporizes some of the intensity of any experience.

"You mean we're *supposed* to throw our arms around like that?"

Extremes in performance style need a long loosening-up rehearsal period to overcome the strangeness. We went quite fully into the whole business of the play which was performed on the show-boat stage. This means 1860 melodrama. It's surprising how they assume, as general audiences do, that the style of acting that they know is the only way it's ever been done, and any other way is strange, funny, peculiar. It does look peculiar, and we actually had great fun practicing the elaborate gestures and vocal flourishes popular until the turn of the century. This was known as elocution. Fortunately, we found a battered old book of recitations and stage gestures, with illustrations; and after some initial puzzlement and timidity, they entered into it and had a good time following the stage directions for *The Famine* by Henry Wadsworth Longfellow. Later in the day they scampered in to report that while they were waiting for the social studies teacher to come in, they repeated their performance, and "everybody loved it."

"Oh, the long and dreary winter..." An 1860 elocution exercise loosens people up.

The period melodrama in *Show Boat* was a splendid opportunity for period acting. Here the melodrama audience files up the gangplank.

An excerpt from
THE FAMINE

By Henry Wadsworth Longfellow
(By permission of Houghton, Mifflin & Co.)

Oh, The Long and Dreary Winter
[Weight upon the back foot…hands tightly clasped, as in struggle.]
Oh, the Cold and Cruel Winter.
[Bring clasped hands to breast, slightly elevating shoulders, and bringing them slightly forward, to suggest a shiver.]
Ever Thicker, Thicker, Thicker,
Froze the Ice on Lake and River,
[Slowly carry weight of body forward until it rests upon the forward foot; raise arms to front, to about the level of waist; then slowly and gracefully carry them out to side, in a descriptive gesture, hands (prone) easily and gracefully held; look around, as if at the frozen waters.]
Ever Deeper, Deeper, Deeper
Fell the Snow O'er All the Landscape,
Fell the covering Snow, and drifted
[Raise both arms (hands hanging relaxed) throughout the first four words, and upon the word "fell," let them begin to descend; depress the upper arm, elbow and wrist, and allow the arms to float downward to little below the level of the shoulders; make a slight gesture stroke upon the word "drifted."]
Through the Forest
[Bring the arms to front, toward one another.]
Round the Village.
[Wave the arms out to side.]

"Would it be too unkind of me to ask you to leave me alone with my schoolroom for a brief moment?" "Oh, no, my dear. 'Tis I who was selfish. I should have known." The melodrama near the beginning.

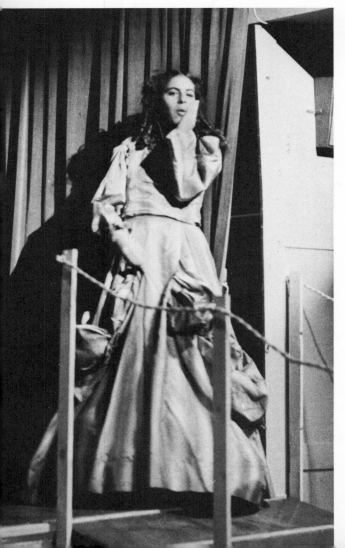

"Who is this evil face confronting our lovely and trembling schoolteacher?" The melodrama narrator makes it clear that the plot has thickened.

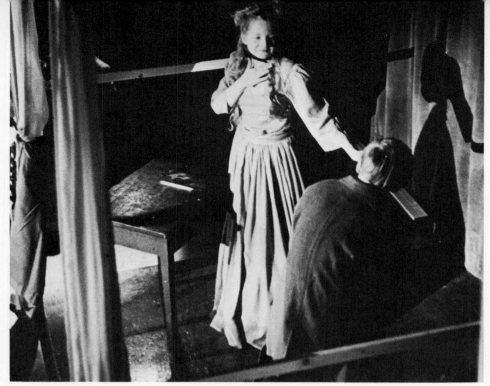

"You may not sully the name of the man I love—a man of God."

We used this only as an exercise and never incorporated it in the performance of *Show Boat*.

This sort of almost-nonsense opens up everybody the way parlor games do. Now the next step is to get them to see that you can behave sincerely, even though your arms and voice fly about at unaccustomed rates.

Here is yet another instance of rehearsal and *then* writing, because the writing of the melodrama began after the first exercises in elocution. After that came the full rehearsal. It's a credit to the students involved that they managed to be convincing and not awkward.

The period that appears to be "just rehearsing" is a valuable time when all the children who are involved in backstage work can feel very important. This is the time for making all aspects of the production mesh, and the time when they learn they must depend on others and must be dependable. Steve and Matthew rehearsed their dockside scene, and worked it over and over until Lori got the entrance with the parasol *just right*. The very morning of the assembly, John and Steve breathlessly got a ladder and put up the *Cotton Blossom* sign. When I had said, "Maybe we can let it go," John said, "Oh, no. We've got to have it for the boat." After the play was over, John came up to tell me all over again how they'd had to rush around to get that sign up.

Faulty light and sound cues can distort the meaning of a dialogue, and the tempo of a curtain can destroy the effect of a scene. We had a near disaster when, at the end of *Young Jefferson*, the lights went down before the last stirring reading from the Declaration of Independence could be started. The audience applauded. Then the child on lights remembered, corrected, brought the lights back up, and they did the final moment. Being deep in the total play, the child was not utterly thrown by one mistake.

Fortunately it looked like a planned effect and was not too distressing. But having the lights correct would have been better. Our lighting system is less than wonderful, and the people on lights have to be in almost total dark, so they cannot follow on the script, and must memorize every cue. It is a great credit to the boys handling the lights for *Show Boat* that lights and sound synchronized.

The interaction of all contributions—no matter how small—stimulates or hinders. Probably this is one of the biggest learnings anyone gets from the production of a play, that each one can say to himself and believe, "When I do something that is just right for my part or for the play, that starts someone else doing better, and that starts someone else, and on and on and on." It's an exciting feeling—the community of interest that makes each job take its rightful creative place. It was nice to hear kids coming off stage after *Show Boat* whispering, "She never did it better…Was it all right?…Oh, that scene with Ila was the strongest in the whole play…."

"I'll go, but I'll be back—don't you worry none."

At this point the melodrama audience gets so engrossed they forget their 1870 reactions.

"There now, my dear. That vulgarity has left us." "Oh, my lovely hero."

D. WHAT DOES THE DIRECTOR DO IF THERE
IS A SLUMP IN INTEREST?

The children are bound to get discouraged, for they don't have the overall view that you have. As director, you must believe in this style of teaching, and the value of this play in particular, and go at it with ebullient determination, for there will be a time when you wonder, "Why did I ever start this?" And when it is over, you will wonder, "How did I ever do it?"

When there is a slump in interest and the children seem to be just repeating themselves, we often add a physical element, such as turning the stage lights on and the house lights off. Or we use in the rehearsals as many costumes and properties as are ready.

During rehearsals for *Show Boat*, when things got low, or people got distracted, there were two sure-fire scenes that would bring the group into focus. One was Liz storming up the aisle as Parthy in "Out Riding with a Murderer." The other was the melodrama. It worked every time. After that we could go on to a more difficult scene, and people would work with the belief that a play really would happen.

Another thing we did, particularly when they seemed to lack spirit, was to run through all the scenes as fast as they could go, with no breaks between. They then got a feeling of the whole story, and how much had really been done. After one such run-through, a little girl said, "I didn't realize our scenes were that good."

Another way of working is to do the scene, or pieces of a scene, over and over till it reaches them. This was particularly true in the miscegenation scene. Anybody gets bored with mechanical repetition, but if the children can see a change for the better, and they themselves are responsible for making it better, and if they have felt their choices accepted or honored all the way along, the repetition will become another chance to make it the way "we want it to be," rather than being an adult requirement.

We try to have a runthrough before a weekend. It keeps their spirits up. At first the play seems to go very slowly, but it picks up momentum and you have no slump problem when you and the children begin to feel the excitement and pressure of the "opening night" deadline.

In the last three days before the assembly program, the cast of *Show Boat* began really making demands on each other—telling each other to be quiet, rehearsing rough spots by themselves, and constantly remembering things that needed to be done.

We are still improvising; not much has been written; and we are not the least bit ready for costuming—but we try some anyway, and this gives them a feeling of how it will look, and something to work toward.

STEP SIX:

Final Rehearsals

A. DURING REHEARSALS, WHEN DO YOU START USING SCENERY, COSTUMES, AND PROPERTIES?

At the expense of wear and tear on the scenery, costumes, and properties, start using them as soon as you can. If something is too valuable, irreplaceable, or consumable, use a substitute during rehearsals up to the last few days. After showing the girls the beautiful black-lace parasol for Magnolia in *Show Boat,* we carefully put it away in plastic until the dress rehearsal. There are bound to be mishaps to properties or costumes in any performance. But no one should go on for the performance wearing clothes and handling objects he has never seen before. Mini-skirted girls need lots of practice to handle hoops and petticoats. When the boy who played sheriff first tried on the long black coat, most of the class laughed and jeered. By the end of a week they had accepted it as part of the character.

Use the stage where this play is to be presented to the school as early as possible, so that the body of each actor gets used to the environment of that stage. Those parts of the set that the actors are going to walk on or work in need to be put up as soon as possible—in other words, construction first, and leave the decoration for later. The two priorities for *Show Boat* were the two gangplanks, and the melodrama stage on the *Cotton Blossom*—the show boat. We tottered up and down those gangplanks for days before we could navigate them easily—and that included us teachers.

Yesterday it was a shallow platform; today it becomes a gangplank.

Above: Concentrating on a light cue.

Left: At first their seams may look like a map of the Mississippi River, but they are learning. Even the melodrama star sews, and the costumes get made.

B. WHO DOES THE PHYSICAL WORK NECESSARY FOR THIS KIND OF PRODUCTION?

Everyone must have *some* part *on* the stage, even though small, and everyone should help with the other work—properties, costumes, lights, etc. The ones with big roles must also do the grubby work. This is essential to eliminate the "star" attitude. It also means that the teacher must do a great deal of organizing. The children need to be taught that organization is essential to the production and that first things come first. Otherwise a project like this, with so many details, will become a mess. On an all-day work session like a holiday or a Saturday, it's a good idea to have everybody meet in one place first, and divide up jobs and people. Crews

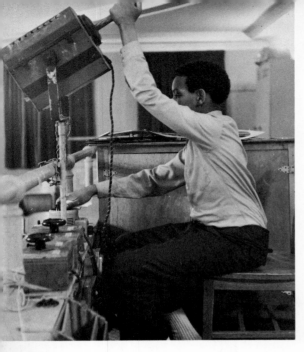

Everybody loves to take a try at lights.

In many cases *we* could do some of these staging jobs faster, but the whole value of the project is that they do these things for themselves.

The way they hammered nails drove us crazy, and we offered suggestions (foolishly). They wanted to do it themselves, and that's right.

Even our leading lady helped sweep and mop.

must get to work early in the process, so that there isn't too much rush at the end. (There will be anyway.) Select *heads* of production crews who probably won't be on the stage most of the time in a long part. It is also better to have many departments than a few with too much to do. This is the way we usually divided up the backstage work:

Assistant Director: watches rehearsals, takes notes, attends to details, keeps a complete script

Production Stage Manager: coordinates all backstage crews; oversees all backstage organization; sees that there is a place for everything and everyone; movement on and off stage is easy; in short, traffic manager

Two Stage Managers: keep script as you move along with the writing; prompt on the day of performance (one from each side of the stage); keep track of people backstage to see that they get on and off easily

Set-Building Crew: use as many as needed—one boy as head

Property Crew: making, gathering, and setting up backstage

Costume Crew: makes preparation, and has the costumes arranged backstage so as to avoid confusion

Sound Effects: can be one of the stage managers

Lights

Program Crew

Planning for an all-day work session.

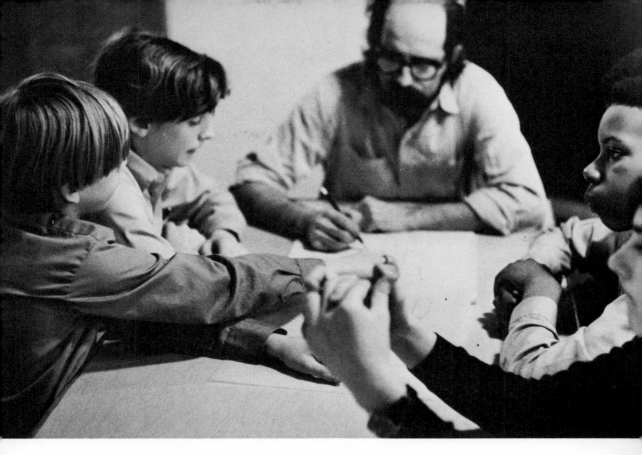

The pilot house for *Show Boat*, from conception...

...through construction...

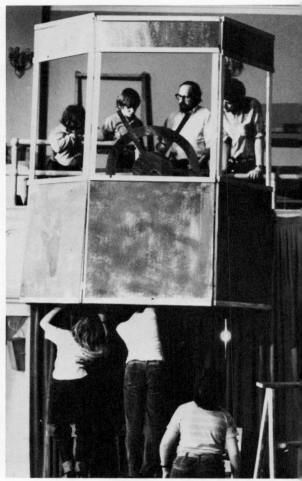

Backstage work is the place where fathers can be a wonderful help with the shop teacher, if you have one, and indispensable if the school has no shop teacher. For one play, mothers brought portable sewing machines and cut and stitched, along with the girls. Parents helping brings the project closer to life outside the school.

We were blessed with a shop teacher who works from design to fabrication, and in *Show Boat*, all we had to do was to wave our arms vaguely and say we wanted a pilot house up there in the balcony. It seemed to appear miraculously, but we know that he and the boys worked down in the shop a long time.

...to consummation.

C. WHEN DO YOU EXPECT THE CHILDREN TO LEARN THE LINES?

There comes a time when everything must be accurately memorized, but with all the previous activity, the memorization comes with meaning, merges with physical behavior on the stage, and they tend to know the total performance rather than mechanically memorized pieces. So, by the time we have gone through all the steps from one to five, everyone knows the play so well that there is comparatively little rehearsal in the traditional sense.

We realized how wise it is to have every scene familiar to many children when Jeff was sick the day of the performance of *Young Jefferson* and José stepped into the part. With notes in his hand, and a quick rehearsal, he managed to play the role—which had some long speeches—well enough for the audience *not to realize the near calamity.*

There were times when kids sitting around watching rehearsal knew the lines better than the children on the stage, and we had to stop them from prompting. For some children, memorizing is a fearful experience, especially when they have to expose themselves on the stage. We constantly remind them, "Think it through and get the sequence of thoughts—don't just memorize blindly." Here is where the assistant director can run through a scene over and over with that child until the lines begin to come easily—a good opportunity for the assistant director.

Scenery, Costumes, & Properties

A. MUST YOU HAVE SCENERY, COSTUMES, AND PROPERTIES?

Costumes are really important, because for the children "dress-up" is essential for acting the story. They have been doing it all their lives. Clothing for a different time or place helps in getting twelve-year-olds, or any actor for that matter, into the part better. Dressing well for an interview may impress the employer but you wear it also because it lifts your sense of yourself. We are not talking of costumes and properties in the traditional sense of being an external piece of decor, but as one of the stimuli in the creative process.

An object in one's hand provides material for the imagination. Girls love to experiment with hair-do's. The night before the performance of *Show Boat* in assembly, the girls all gathered at a home where the mother knew how to put up curls with rags. They came to school next morning with mixed pleasure and embarrassment, but their hair was beautiful. Get pictures of the period and let them copy and admire each other. A night stick can make a boy talk more like a policeman. Matthew really wanted a walking stick for Ravenal in *Show Boat* and went backstage and found one. Girls with gloves on for party scenes can muster a more ladylike behavior.

Robert goes through all sorts of books on history and costumes, and becomes our authority on clothes of the period.

It's easier to spread out on the floor when you want to look at several reference books.

Some of the books we have used for suggestions about clothing and household articles are:

Playing Period Plays by Lyn Oxenford
Godey's Lady Book
Currier and Ives prints
Copies of old illustrated schoolbooks and novels
Colonial Living by Edwin Tunis

This search for things that are appropriate to the character, time, or place enlarges the awareness of the world. It sharpens the capacity for observation, and to be able to observe accurately makes one better at any job. Using objects suitable to a character—a pocket watch, a cane, a hat, or a pair of gloves—helps a child stand in that person's shoes, so to speak, and helps him understand the character's thinking and feeling. *Understanding* is even more important than play-acting in the development of the child, and the end result is inevitably more vivid for the audience.

An item which is the merest suggestion of a period or character is often enough, but it is the judicious choice of that item that matters. The child must find a quality in the character, and then find something that makes him feel more like that quality than before he used the property or clothing. For instance, in the play about the colonial boy with the injured hand, it helped the boy who played the role to have on clothes that were dirty and ragged for the scenes after he had burned his hand and felt alone and homeless. We even bound up his hand in dirty strips of sheeting. However, John Hancock in the same play couldn't help feeling elegant with his starched white ruffles and gold-headed cane.

Costumes and props need not be expensive or complete. It's the searching that intensifies the character. Just a coat with brass buttons can *feel* like a uniform.

The parasol for Magnolia.

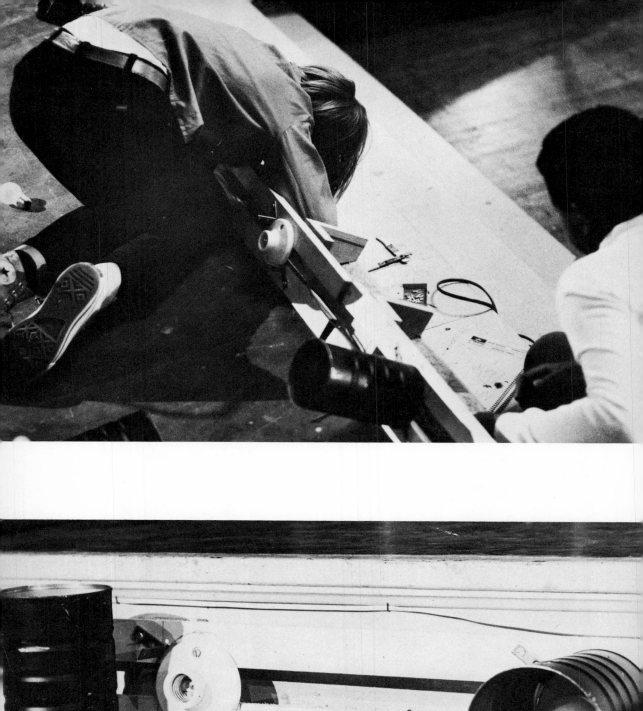

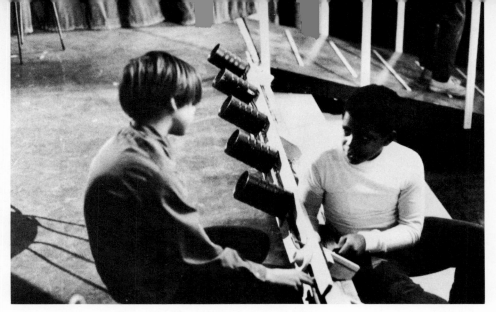

Another staging triumph—the footlights for the *Show Boat* melodrama.

B. HOW MUCH SCENERY DO YOU HAVE TO HAVE?

For a number of reasons, we have always kept our scenery and properties simple—down to the barest essentials. It's a matter of priorities. There's no need even to have walls. Make a lightweight frame the size and shape of doors and windows, drape the windows for the period of the setting, and often that is enough. Too elaborate a set takes away from the simplicity and spirit of the children's work, which is our first concern.

Furniture against drapes or against a bare wall is often more effective than furniture painted on a backdrop. Settle for an old table from the junk yard rather than a painted imitation. You want something only here and there to create an illusion. If you are fortunate enough to have stage lights, experiment with them to give an effect of outdoors, or a lamp-lit room. The boys and the shop teacher used #10 juice cans to simulate foot lights for all of *Show Boat,* and particularly for the melodrama. Footlights are very old-fashioned, and give a special effect.

Because we have never had a "real stage," we have never had a front curtain, and now the most modern theaters have caught up with us, and use no front curtain. Even those theaters that are traditionally equipped often do not use a curtain between the acts. Scenery is changed in full view of the audience, either in dim light or with all the lights on. Sometimes people dressed for the period of the play can do the changing, and make a pleasant little interlude of the operation. Modern directors realize that the audience doesn't need a curtain to create the illusion that what happens on the stage is truth. Scenes in *Show Boat,* on the deck, in Julie's room, and Parthy's sitting room were all staged with the melodrama stage in full view across the back, and everyone accepted it. The aisles in the audience were paths down to the dock.

We tend to use the aisles more and more because it brings actors and audience closer together. It has become very popular in the theater, and like most schools, we don't have an adequate backstage. Don't let handicaps like that stop you.

C. WHERE DO YOU GET SCENERY, COSTUMES, AND PROPERTIES?

You can begin by getting the children to read supplementary books, especially fiction, to steep them in the atmosphere of the period and situation. In books they will find references to clothing and objects commonly used, such as quill pens, ladies' needlework, the straight slatback chairs of the Puritans, etc. There are many books available that show pictures of household objects as well as tools and clothing. There are even reprints of old books of etiquette. Reproductions of paintings teach a great deal about a period. If you are interested in this way of combining social studies and drama, it would pay to start a collection of pictures from magazines, Christmas cards, and art books.

If you are very lucky, there will be a re-run on television of a movie set in the very period of the play you are working on. Sometimes historical inaccuracies in movies have to be gone over the next day in school, but it is well worth it, for the interest that the movie generates.

The Patriots by Sidney Kingsley would help you get a feeling for Thomas Jefferson, the man, even though it's about his later life. *Saratoga Trunk* is an old film we should have shown for preparing *Show Boat*. The costumes were of that period. *Washington Square* as a novel was good for some students who could read Henry James, and the movie made from it, *The Heiress*, would interest everybody, and it gave a period setting. Lots of westerns depict this period in a different locale.

Perhaps we should explain why we don't take our youngsters to movies that are dramatizations of stories on which we are working. It is because they are done by people who have a great deal more experience than our seventh and eighth graders have; and it tends to discourage our novice playwrights or make them slavish copyists.

Trips can be planned to get firsthand experiences with materials for properties. Fortunately, we lived surrounded by restorations and museums of the colonial and Revolutionary period, so it was easy to combine history, drama, art, and English on our trips. The day we went to the American Wing of the Metropolitan Museum of New York, it became not just a museum tour but an enthusiastic search for the way the stage should look and what clothes were appropriate for the play they were doing. They felt the need of finding accurate information in order to make their play the way they wanted it to be.

Sometimes the opportunities for trips will help you decide which story to choose for dramatization. This is one of the very important parts of the project—that you help them to reach out and relate their own lives with times past.

Often parents can play a valuable part in searching out information and things to use. It was a special moment for the cast of *Show Boat* when Mady brought the news that her grandmother had known a little girl in Missouri who had really lived on a show boat. Somebody's mother can turn a discarded pair of drapes into a wonderful colonial skirt, or Patrick Henry's knee breeches can be made of cut-off regular trousers. But get the class to do as much as *they* can and not depend too much on their mothers. Children who live in the country are lucky; they or their neighbors will have attics or cellars or big closets full of old clothes and furniture.

We were struggling over which sash to put on a dress, and Mady said, "I wish people could know how much work goes into making one small thing just right."

"Oh, how lovely—can we use it?"

"Here's a blouse to go with the skirt. Is this 1870?"

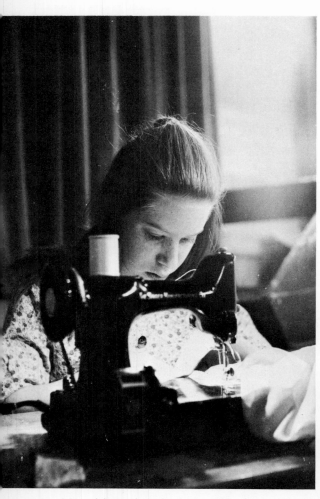

Most of the work can be done on the sewing machine...

...but sometimes you have to sew each other in.

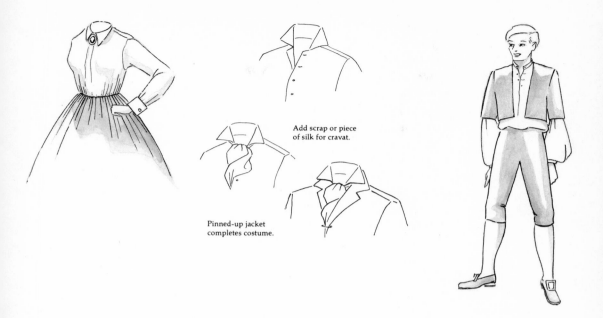

Add scrap or piece
of silk for cravat.

Pinned-up jacket
completes costume.

As we've said before, don't try for a complete set. Also, we never have *rented* an entire set, and we don't intend to ever. And we think you should not. Furniture can almost always be borrowed, and lightweight lumber can be bought fairly inexpensively for door and window frames. We have been known to use pieces of packing boxes, and any number of other things picked up here and there.

One of the instructive, and amusing, things about using current "old clothes" and other things that you dig out of closets and attics is that you discover that clothes from any period are in some way like some other period. For example, here are some of the things we did to costume a Civil War period play:

The cotton shirtwaist dresses of the 1950's that are again back in style became Civil War dresses by the addition of high collars and pantalettes, the latter made by fastening small petticoats by elastic bands above each knee, so that they hung down to just above the ankle. Men's suits for the same period can be simulated simply by closing any dark suit up close to the neck by a safety pin; turning a white shirt collar up like a wing collar; and then adding a silk scarf or just a piece of satin across the front, tucking it into the coat like a cravat for a tie.

For the Victorian Prince Albert coat of the Civil War and later periods, a lady's fitted coat shortened appropriately and worn with dark trousers does very well. Civil War uniforms of either side are much more difficult, but a few red stripes and brass buttons can do much. Military peaked caps are virtually impossible. So, if you can't rent—and you probably shouldn't—try to arrange it so that the gentlemen can be seen without hats or only holding them.

As for young boys of this period, many of them wore trousers fitted tight and ending just below the knee. Take any cotton trousers that are slightly outgrown, and seam them in to fit the calf. Now add a lady's white or light-blue blouse with a Peter Pan collar, and for a jacket, a lady's bolero, shortened to about the level of the elbow. This gives quite an authentic impression.

The very elegant ladies of this period wore very full skirts, with hoops. Some ingenious person may be able to construct hoops for you, but the full skirts are the most important and they are the delight of both the girls and their parents. Consult history books and illustrations for *Little Women* and *Lady Book,* and go to work with old bedspreads, couch covers, lace and organdy curtains, and drapes. We ourselves have contributed full-skirted, floor-length house coats. A skirt is easiest to make—just stitch together three panels of ankle length and gather for the waist by running elastic through a top hem. Tops are much more difficult, so don't make them, but find silk or cotton dress tops or jackets to which you can add some of the skirt material as trim to bring the two together.

The other historic period in which we have had some experience is the colonial through Revolutionary period. In general, color helps to give a feeling of any period. Obviously, the Pilgrims and Puritans used black, brown, and gray. The working class of all colonies tended to dress in homespun, home-dyed cloth, in whatever colors were available to them. They dyed with beet root, berries, and tree bark and often used the natural colors of the wool or hemp. The gentry used richer colors and materials, which they could afford to have imported from the Orient and Europe.

To costume the Puritans and Pilgrims, start with ladies' or men's dark shirts or blouses, and add collars and cuffs, cut from worn out white sheets or from paper, although paper is so perishable that it is scarcely worth it. Let the girls look at pictures, cut paper patterns until they get the desired effect, and then cut the sheets. They don't even need to be hemmed if time is short, although spray starch and a good pressing helps a great deal. Skirts may be a problem; you may have to buy cheap material that looks somewhat like the blouses. Make floor-length gathered skirts. Don't bother with a waist band; just run elastic through the top hem. It makes the costume much more adjustable if you have to make changes or if you want to use it again. Remember that old sheets can be dyed any color you want because they take cold-water dyes like Tintex or Rit so well.

Workingmen's and artisans' costumes are best made by taking modern clothing of somewhat the right color and shape and tearing it to make it look worn and ragged. For the most part, these people were poor. Cloth was dear and time-consuming to weave and make into clothes, so they wore things until they were in shreds. Incidentally, this is the kind of knowledge of history you pass along to youngsters as you send them out searching for their clothing.

For the women of this class, put two long, full skirts over each other. Then pull the hem of the outer one up on the sides and tuck it in at the waist. Sometimes an apron over this helps. For the blouses use men's shirts from which you rip the collars and cuffs. Dye them with Tintex—any color that does not match the skirt—roll the sleeves up, tuck the neck in, and you have a costume something like the women in the paintings of Breughel or Vermeer, especially if you use a head kerchief tied back under the hair.

It's almost as easy to make men's and boys' clothing for this period. Use old brown or gray trousers, several sizes too large for the actor, so they will be baggy. Cut them off a few inches belòw the knee, tuck them into knee-length socks, cinch the waist in with cord, belt, or even strips of cloth. Now get a man's

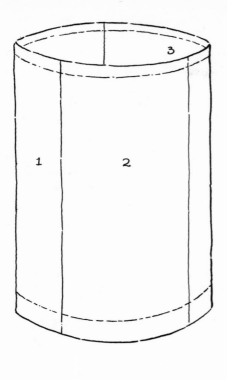

Stitch together 3 panels of
ankle length and gather at waist
by running elastic through top hem.

shirt—any color other than white will do, as snowy white linen was the mark of a gentleman—cut off collar and cuffs, and roll and tuck as you did for the women. Now cut the sleeves completely out of a man's old brown or gray suit jacket or hip-length outdoor coat. You may even cut off the lower edge and fray it so that it looks worn, or perhaps pull out the lining, and with the shirt tucked in or hanging out, depending on the character, and the sleeveless overjacket, you have a colonial workman's outfit.

Shoes for both men and women can be any heavy shoes or the currently popular moccasin, with foil-covered buckles attached to give money status. As we write this, the most popular shoes for men and women are perfect for colonial costumes—save them! Now richer people's clothes are more a matter of building, rather than pulling apart. Gentlemen's breeches can be made in the same way as the workers, except that they should fit a little tighter, be a little brighter in color, or good black, and they should have buckles added at the knees. Tights or white stockings and buckles on the shoes complete the lower part. The shirts don't show much, so all you have to do is concoct a neckcloth by wrapping anything white like a handkerchief or strip of white sheet around the neck. Add to it a ruffle or jabot made of the same material, or lace if you can find it (we have been known to use Kleenex in a desperate backstage emergency). For the coat

Shoes circa 1969.

One of the most important parts of a project like this is that teachers confer, keep in touch, and constantly work with each other. It's good for the kids to see adults working together the same way *they* are expected to.

use a woman's fitted coat either from a suit or a dress coat which you can turn up or cut off midway between the hip and knee. Add a double row of buttons down the front. Ruffles and buttons go on the cuffs. The traditional tricorn you can easily make from somebody's old felt hat. The waistcoat, an elaborate affair in George Washington's day, can be eliminated, or if you can find a brocaded-looking or flowered dress made in princess lines and buttoned down the front, cut out the sleeves, shorten the skirt, cut the neck down, or fold it in to get the waistcoat line, and you have it.

One word of warning! When you send out the word that you want old clothes for costumes be sure that it's not just the *children's* decisions that you may have a garment to cut up. Get an okay from the parents. It's a great way for kids to get rid of clothes they hate.

But, it is delightful when they work together. It's a nice feeling for kids to see all the grown-ups pitching in and working together.

None of us really knows what a show boat looks like. So students are dispatched to the library to look in history books, picture books, and even novels for pictures of the period.

D. HOW CAN YOU GET ALL THIS DONE IN SCHOOL TIME?

Don't think for a minute that you can hold on to the customary classroom routines during final rehearsals. Until then, the reading, improvisation, planning, and writing can be done during regular scheduled class time, with occasional after-school sessions. In the final excitement we spend a good deal of energy running to other teachers adjusting time. It isn't "wasted" time, however. Many routine assignments and discussions in social studies and English can be left out because the learning is taking place while developing many aspects of the production. For some years we were very fortunate that English and social studies were both taught by the homeroom teacher, and the children went twice a week for drama classes to a drama teacher. It will take more organization if more teachers are working on the project, but it may have great advantages. In every situation there will be problems of schedule and the pressure of academic needs. Don't let this discourage you. Even though your situation may be different from ours, you can still use this technique.

Remember that the class learns more vividly and permanently the very subjects you had planned to teach in the curriculum, because it is coupled with the intense emotional experience of this play. This is the advantage in choosing for dramatization a book that deals with the history your class is studying.

Some of the English we are sure the children learned:

(a) The correct form for dramatic writing. That is, it must be written in the first person, and must be written in the present tense.
(b) Distinction between direct and indirect quotation.
(c) The form and punctuation of dialogue.
(d) The need to realize words of another time and place. This is sometimes called "style" or "usage." One class dealt with the flowery language of the melodrama in the play *Show Boat*.
(e) Growth of vocabulary and more precise meaning of words.
(f) How to give and take directions.
(g) The need for content—a message, an idea—to give to the audience. They begin to look for themes in all literature.
(h) Improvement of grammar and style—verbs make a story move.
(i) Improvement in spelling.
(j) Rules of punctuation.

Some of the ways they expanded their knowledge of history:

(a) In order to write a play at all, set in any historic period, you have to find out a great deal more than you would need to know in order to answer questions on a classroom test. You can get a sense of a different life style of a period if the social-studies class is used for an exploration of the way of living for the time of the setting of the play. In *Show Boat*, the racial situation, so heartrendingly felt by Julie, socially and economically, is a springboard for much study of the black man's position after the Civil War. Was it as difficult on plantations, and in the crowded cities like New Orleans? Was the ex-slave free? How "free" were the poor whites?

97

(b) They began to feel the need for more exact information at times. One class learned the exact wording of the Declaration of Independence. In deciding how much of the Declaration we needed for the opening chorus, and then which parts could be used for choral speaking interludes between each scene, the seventh graders dug into the Declaration to find out what it really said. They wanted to quote those lines which the scene to follow would exemplify. Seldom has a social-studies period included such intensive thinking and discussion of a formidable document. "All men are created equal" became a wonderful beginning when they had read the whole Declaration and saw that it was the basic theme for this book and play.

A project on the Mississippi river valley was appropriate for *Show Boat*. By the time we read the first chapter of the book, the children knew that Kim was named for Kentucky, Illinois, and Missouri, because she was born at the point where the three states meet. A map of the whole area with the river towns put on it would make river life more clear.

The amount and importance of shipping then and now, and the types of boats, is another area of facts that would interest children. There is a vivid section about Mississippi River boatmen and the cargoes the boats carried, in *We the People* by Leo Huberman (Harper, 1947). And *Life on the Mississippi* by Mark Twain has an even fuller description. Carl Carmer's *Rome Haul* is an exciting book for good readers. It is set in the Mohawk Valley in New York, but the river life was similar to that on the Mississippi.

The business of transportation in the United States would be a big project and would bring in the development of roads and of railroads as well as river travel, and this would be valuable in understanding any of the American historical plays.

"Cotton was king in show boat days." They need to find out what that slogan meant. The problem of producing cotton, shipping it, and getting it manufactured into cloth makes a project involving economics and politics as well as much of the social life of the different classes.

(c) They saw the need for a wealth of detail essential to really understanding an incident or person. There are many factors in, and causes for, an event. For example, in *Johnny Tremain,* they learned, in a way they won't forget, the first battle of the Revolution by knowing the people—Paul Revere, Dr. Warren, Sam Adams, John Hancock, Sons of Liberty, and others who were active in Boston. So also there are various ways of learning about the Stamp Act and the Boston Tea Party. The kind of government that controlled the people—or against whom they fought, as in *Johnny Tremain*—provides a project with interesting questions. Who was King of England at the time? Or in other settings, who was president? Who was governor? How many states were there then?

(d) They learned to use many sources to get information—texts, reference books, pictures, trips, maps, documents.

(e) They became acquainted with some aspects of cultural differences often not noted in textbooks. For instance, they had to deal with the many problems of racial intermarriage one hundred years ago, and talk about what small gains had been made since then.

One of the final touches—measuring drapes.

(f) They learned to organize material to convey an idea they wanted to communicate.

(g) They learned to polish and perfect a statement.

This they were willing to do in order to make a character communicate the idea clearly. That's the way they worked on the Declaration of Independence. Yes, they got a lot of academic information, but they grew as people, and that matters more.

(a) They learned to listen to each other, especially during the writing of scenes.

(b) They learned to "fight" and then compromise for the sake of the production.

(c) They learned that people whom they considered unimportant may have fabulous contributions to make.

(d) They learned that this way of performing is an illuminating way, and this gives them more respect for unorthodox ways of learning.

(e) They learned that "hard work" can be a joy and very satisfying. The master builder of a piece of scenery one year stood smiling at it and said, "I love it. I wish I could take it home."

(f) They learned the reality of taking on responsibility themselves.

(g) They learned—even if they were not aware of it at the time—that to think together and to put that thought into physical action for a social purpose, binds people in lifelong relationships.

We feel safe in assuming that they did experience some of these growths, because they themselves talked about them at a breakfast meeting. "One of the things was that when things went wrong in rehearsal we ran to the teacher, but when we played the real performances we had to take things on ourselves."

A classroom teacher can help the children work out a charming, sensitive scene keeping to classroom schedule and not using other teachers. But the achievement lacks some of the social values and personal development that the extended project can produce. The very bigness of the project did something very important for our performers.

There will always have to be some classes adhered to, such as math or science, if these subjects are not involved in the play. At the junior high school age, the children need the stabilizing influence of some classroom routines. Concentrating all day on a project such as the play is too taxing.

The drapes were used for the small melodrama stage on the *Cotton Blossom*.

STEP EIGHT:

The Performance

A. CAN YOU RELY ON THIS METHOD TO GET A PERFORMANCE THAT INTERESTS THE WHOLE HIGH SCHOOL AS MUCH AS YOU CAN BY A MORE USUAL METHOD?

For us it's only by drawing on the very real inner selves of the children that something moving and genuine happens.

This way of working, in which there usually is a great deal of disorder, does actually result in a performance of vitality and conviction. This way produces a play with more spirit and inner truth than does a method of just learning lines. A school assembly or an adult audience can't help sensing that difference.

You can see by the many steps that we went through, that this is a long involved experience. But even if the performance were not so interesting to the audience, which it was, this process is worth while to the children. At a breakfast meeting one of the girls said, "You had to have that feeling really in you. You can read in any social studies book how a person felt, and understand how they felt. But, to dramatize it, boy, you had to get that feeling inside yourself, so you could produce it for the audience."

And another year one said, "When I think about last year, I can't remember what was history and what was drama."

And one of the boys said, "You have to research hard. It's like hypnotizing yourself. You have to look it up, all the aspects that are good, and what happened. Finally, you're just *in* the thing."

This meant to us that we had succeeded. It has invariably resulted for us in a deeper, richer performance that often surprises the audience.

Junior high school children, who are at a very tentative and changeable stage of their lives, have assumed many adult standards for themselves that they are not fully able to live up to. They often want to put on adult plays. They want to appear grown-up, and in copying that appearance without understanding its source, they manage to seem only unreal. Using this technique of writing their own plays and developing the emotional content of the scenes brings them closer to the desirable adult standards than they get by imitating the surface appearance of adults.

Part of your success will come from choosing a story which is mature enough to challenge both you and the children, and yet not too difficult for them to absorb emotionally. Choose books with strong problems and statements. Children want to belong to the world, and they can grasp truly great themes. However, although Shakespeare and George Bernard Shaw are great playwrights and their themes are universal, their plays are, for the most part, beyond the capacity of the children to identify with and enjoy acting. The implications in such sophisticated writing are too complex for even bright children of this age to perform. They may be quite able to read it and understand it. Performing it is a different and more difficult matter. The children need to *write* their own scenes and struggle with expressing the deep emotions that they themselves are aware of.

B. HOW DO YOU KEEP CHILDREN FROM BEING NERVOUS BEFORE AN AUDIENCE?

In spite of the work that has gone into the production so far, and the understanding on the part of each one, the moment of appearing before an audience is frightening as well as exhilarating. But having been on the stage in the working process of writing and rewriting, each one feels more at ease on the stage when the whole play is run through, and because of this can face an audience with less terror on the part of the shy and with less exhibitionism on the part of the show-off. Even those who had to step in at the last minute seemed to fit in and have the same sense of proportion without self-consciousness.

The sense of the whole, through having written the play and the experience of working together, sustains them. This kind of preparation keeps children from going to pieces when mistakes occur, because their minds are more on the play than on themselves. A child can be so wrapped up in a character that he can use different words from the prepared script, and yet not throw off other characters. He can paraphrase the written speech so well that he doesn't realize that he's made a change, and, for that matter, neither do the other children on the stage. Everybody knew that Ila changed the words of the final scene every time she rehearsed, but it didn't bother them. They were entranced, by the character and the situation. This is not acceptable when performing Shakespeare, but it's almost inevitable for productions that come from improvisations. The best of modern actors use something of this improvisational approach. There is a sudden quality of life in an improvisation that always appeals to an audience. It's admittedly taxing in the process of preparation.

Of course there's a quality of breathless excitement at "curtain time." This is a sign of the success of this process of learning. Wouldn't any teacher welcome such interest and excitement in a classroom session? Don't tell them *not* to be excited. Help them to use it. We often say to them, "Yes, I know you're scared, but we have something important to tell that audience. So let's get on the stage and make it like the best rehearsal we've ever had." We have seldom had a child break up and get the giggles in the midst of a performance, even when the audience has made it difficult for the actors.

C. WHY BOTHER WITH THIS TIME-CONSUMING METHOD?

Although it may seem like taking a lot of time, it is worth it because of all the things they learn in a variety of areas. Bits of disconnected knowledge need to have context and continuity. Here we have a chance to relate them in an emotional way with great satisfaction at the end, which seems to batten down many of the bits of information acquired during the process of production. A person might

The play is over. They bow in pretty good unison. The applause is gratifying.

know parts of the Declaration of Independence "by heart," but these children knew how it grew, and lived through the situation that produced it. They really understand it, now, whether they can now quote all of it exactly or not. With our fun and nonsense over the melodrama in *Show Boat,* the eighth grade probably has a lasting impression of one aspect of the Victorian period. Putting on a performance before an audience is a slight achievement in comparison to the growth and learning that takes place in this long project.

D. WHEN THE PERFORMANCE IS OVER, HOW DO YOU GET THEM TO SETTLE DOWN TO REGULAR CLASSROOM ROUTINES?

The children have been at a high pitch and need discussion to evaluate their experiences in the play, and giving it discussion time will help to solidify the learning. In such a discussion, you can allay fears about their mistakes, and audience reactions, and find ways to show that the small contributions do count. Let them indulge in a little well-earned pride. A success of this kind in the early adolescent years is a steppingstone toward a feeling of confidence in facing the uncertain world ahead of them.

Try to have some appealing, short, related projects planned for the classroom work, to hold the zest for hard work they have built up during the play. Some ideas for this:

(a) Write letters to people outside the classroom who helped in the performance or even to the author of the book they dramatized.
(b) Take each historic character from the play, and follow him along in history beyond the climax of the play.
(c) Read other novels about the period you have been working on. For instance, for the American Revolution, read *Valley Forge* by Maxwell Anderson. For the Civil War period, read *Harriet* by Colin Clemens, or *Abe Lincoln in Illinois* by Robert Sherwood.

We think that, though they "settle down" eventually, their feeling about "learning" has changed a little, and their attitude toward each other has become more receptive.

We have mentioned our traditional Sunday-morning breakfast meeting sometime after the play is over. We tape part of the play, and let them hear themselves and in general enjoy going back over the play. These are some of their reactions we've picked up through the years:

"The play started me off on a whole new phase."

"I didn't think I had stage fright during the performance, whenever I sat down, I wasn't nervous, but when I stood up, my knees shook."

"Let's do it again."

"Debbie, who was in it only three days, was just as happy as we were."

"Throughout the whole play, I kept wishing we were older, and could do more with it."

"It might not have meant anything to the audience, but I think it meant a lot to our class. We had been working on it for so long it couldn't help but mean something to us."

"In the Public Day scene in Williamsburg, everyone was gathered around in the party just talking, and every time we did it, it sounded as if it were too modern, so we had to put it back a few years."

"I heard that last line, it sounded so...Well, I started crying."

"Oh, I got chills over it. I'm getting chills now just thinking about it."

"At the end of the play, Debbie and I just stood there for a minute, and then we began hugging each other." "It helped give our class status in the whole school. Everybody walked in saying, 'Oh, the eighth grade is going to put on a play.' There's a barrier between eighth grade and the rest of the grades, because they're in high school, and we're junior high. If the play had turned out worse, we'd have been worse off. But since it turned out so good, they couldn't believe that we were doing it."

But even after the project is over they love to talk about its difficulties and satisfactions—as they do here at a Sunday breakfast meeting.

Our Script for Show Boat

*Show Boat**

SCENE I: PILOT HOUSE

ANDY: Captain here—more steam!

MAGNOLIA: Why is it so wavy?

PILOT: Squally weather.

MAGNOLIA: *(Pointing)* What's that?

ANDY: What's what?

MAGNOLIA: That over there.

PILOT: A house⎫
ANDY: A barn ⎭ *(at same time)*

MAGNOLIA: No, not the house, the red thing in the water.

PILOT: That's a channel marker.

MAGNOLIA: May I help steer the boat?

PILOT: You steer and I'll help you. Magnolia, you're steering the wrong way. Besides it's beginning to get rough here. I had better take her now.

MAGNOLIA: Oh all right. (Pause) Why is the water that color?

PILOT: Well, you see, at night the man in the moon drops yellow dye down.

MAGNOLIA: You're teasing me. Is it really true?

*Remember that this script is given here only as an example—it would be of little educational value to have your students use it instead of reading a novel and making up their own play. In any case, neither this script nor any other derived from Show Boat can be performed without written permission.

Gaylord Ravenal.

109

PILOT: Would I tease you?

MAGNOLIA: Well...I don't...

PARTHY: MAGNOLIA!

MAGNOLIA: *(In a whisper)* Don't tell her I'm here. *(Ducks out of sight)*

PARTHY: Andy Hawks, is that girl with you? She ought to be like other girls, going to school—not hanging around the wild life on boats.

ANDY: Now leave her alone! She just went down to the cook's quarters.

PARTHY: I'm sure! Maggy has her arithmetic lesson now, and she is not allowed to miss it. Do you hear me?

MAGNOLIA: *(Rising up)* I don't want to go to my arithmetic lesson. I want to stay here!

PARTHY: Magnolia, I'm counting to ten and you had better scoot on down here or I will come up. Andy Hawks, I want to have a word with you later.

ANDY: Now listen, Parthenia...Oh, forget it? *(Under his breath)* Damnation.

MAGNOLIA: All right, I'm coming.

(At this point Andy and the pilot continue steering in the pilot house and talking together while Parthenia stalks up and down the stage, then plants herself firmly in a chair beside the table where Magnolia is to do her lessons. This gives Magnolia time to go down behind the pilot house, and make her entrance on the main stage)

Scene I, continued: Math Lesson

(Maggie enters in a sulk)

MAGNOLIA: I don't want to do arithmetic.

PARTHY: Arithmetic is much better than wasting time in the pilot house. *(Parthy sits Maggy in chair)*

PARTHY: I do declare, Maggy Hawks, if you hang around the pilot house much longer, you'll never be a well-bred young lady. Now...what's nine times seven?

MAGNOLIA: *(Thinks)*...fifty-six.

PARTHY: No, that's seven times eight. And I'll thank you to look at the book and not out the window. Since you know seven times eight, what's eight times eight?

MAGNOLIA: Fifty-six.

PARTHY: Just because fifty-six was the answer for seven times eight does not mean it is the answer to eight times eight. I declare, Maggy Hawks, sometimes you're downright simple. You ought to know more at the age of twelve.

MAGNOLIA: I don't care what eight times eight is! Elly doesn't know either. I asked her and she said she didn't know eight of anything or eight times anything. Elly is the most beautiful person in the world, except me when I smile, and she doesn't know it, so why should I!

PARTHY: If you talk to me like that again, Maggie Hawks, I'll smack you just as sure as I'm sitting here!

MAGNOLIA: It's Magnolia...Magnolia! Um...something beautiful—I don't know what—but not Hawks!

PARTHY: *(Clapping Magnolia's forehead)* My goodness, child, no wonder! You have a fever! Off to bed with you, and I'll put a cold compress on your head!

(Lights dim out)

SCENE 2: MISCEGENATION

(Julie and Steve in cabin, Julie sitting propped up on pillows in bed. Elly knocks)

ELLY: Julie, Julie? Are you there? Julie, I'm going into town. Do you want me to get you something?

JULIE: No. I just want to be left alone. *(Turns face into pillows)*

(Parthy and Maggie enter)

PARTHY: I don't understand this. How did you get sick so sudden? Maggie, go and get some tea and honey for her.

ELLY: You sure you don't want anything? An orange, maybe, or something from the drugstore?

JULIE: No. No.

STEVE: Give her room to breathe.

ELLY: Are you sure, Julie?

PARTHY: Elly, I insist you leave. You're disturbing Julie.

(Elly leaves)

PARTHY: If she's so sick, she needs a doctor. I insist on a doctor.

STEVE: I'm her husband. If she needs or wants a doctor, I'll get her one.

PARTHY: Sir. May I inform you that I own this boat. And I say, a doctor.

STEVE: You own this boat? Andy Hawks owns this boat.

PARTHY: The fact is, she is sick and needs a doctor.

(Maggie comes in with tea and honey)

PARTHY: Maggie, don't get too near Julie. It may be contagious. Maggie, did you hear what I said? Go sit in that chair in the back.

MAGGIE: No, I want to be next to Julie.

PARTHY: Maggie, leave the room.

(Maggie leaves. Andy and Doc enter)

ANDY: Are you going to be able to play tonight, Julie?

JULIE: No. I can't play tonight.

DOC: You sure about that, Julie? Are you really that sick? How long you think you'll be out?

JULIE: Please don't ask me questions. Steve, please tell them to leave me alone.

STEVE: All right. Everybody out.

(Maggie runs in)

MAGGIE: Julie! Julie! They took your pictures down from the billboard. Are you ever going to play again?

PARTHY: *(Taking Doc aside and speaking quietly)* It's kind of strange, all this. I remember last year Julie was sick in this same town.

DOC: It does seem strange.

ANDY: I don't know. It could be the climate. I don't feel too well myself.

PARTHY: Well, I may not know much, but—

ANDY: *(Interrupting)* Don't be so suspicious, woman. *(Turning back to the bed)* You sure you can't play by tonight, Julie?

(Sound of heavy footsteps)

WINDY: *(Stands at door)* Seems that skunk Pete's up to something. He yanked the picture out of the hall. I seen him.

STEVE: I'll kill him this time.

(Steve lunges for the door. All the men rush to stop him and there is a short scuffle)

WINDY: I seen you take the first picture, Steve.

STEVE: I didn't. I never did.

JULIE: Why would he want to steal a picture of his own wife?

WINDY: So nobody in this town would see it, Julie. Fifty years piloting on the river you have to have pretty good eyesight. Mine's as good today as it was when I was twenty. I just came down to warn you I seen Pete coming along with Ike Keener. Ike's the sheriff. He'll be here any minute.

ANDY: Let him. What do we have to worry about? Our license is paid. Sheriff's welcome on this boat as anybody.

(Julie clings to Steve. Steve holds her tight first, then loosens his hold and takes out a pocket knife. The women scream, but Julie does not. Andy jumps at Steve)

STEVE: I'm not going to hurt her, you fool. Let me be! I know what I'm doing. *(Pounding at the door to the boat)* Someone go down and keep him there a minute. It won't hurt much, darling.

(Steve makes a small cut on Julie's forefinger, bends his head down, and sucks the blood. Then he quickly puts his knife in his pocket. Then the sheriff comes in)

SHERIFF: Who's captain of this here boat?

ANDY: *(Walking over to sheriff)* I am. What's wanted with him? Hawks is my name. Captain Andy Hawks. Twenty years on the river.

SHERIFF: Well, Captain. Kind of unpleasant, but there's a miscegenation case on board.

MAGGIE: What? What's that? What does he mean?

PARTHY: Hush now, Maggie.

ANDY: What's that you're speaking of?

SHERIFF: Miscegenation. Case of a Negro woman married to a white man. Criminal offense in this state, as you well know.

ANDY: No such thing on board my boat.

(Elly enters)

SHERIFF: Name of the white man is Steve Baker. Name of Negress...name of the Negress is Julie Dozier. Which ones is them?

ELLY: Oh, my God. Oh, my God. Oh, my God.

SHULTZY: Shut up!

STEVE: I'm Steve Baker. This is my wife, Julie Baker.

SHERIFF: You two better get dressed and come along with me.

(Julie stands up. Steve puts his arm around her)

STEVE: You wouldn't call a man a white man that's got Negro blood in him, would you?

SHERIFF: No, I wouldn't. Not here in Mississippi. One drop of nigger blood makes you a nigger here in these parts.

STEVE: Well then. I got more than one drop of Negro blood in me. And that's a fact. You can't make miscegenation out of that.

SHERIFF: You ready to swear to that in a court of law?

STEVE: I'll swear to it any place. I'll swear to it now. I'll do more than that. Look at all these folks here. There ain't one of them but can swear I got Negro blood in me this minute. That's how white I am.

SHERIFF: Well, I seen fairer men than you was niggers. Still, you better tell that...

WINDY: Guess you've known me, Ike, better part of twenty-five years. I was piloting, time you was runnin' round, barefoot on the landin'. Now I'm telling you—me, Windy McLain—that that "white" man there has got nigger blood in him. I'll take my oath on that.

SHERIFF: If it was anybody else but Windy...*(Stops and thinks)*...But I got this information straight from somebody ought to know.

ANDY: From who? From a sooty-faced scab of a bull-drumming engineer named Pete. And why? Because he's been stuck on Julie, I don't know how long, and she wouldn't have anything to do with him.

SHERIFF: Is that right?

STEVE: Yes, it is. He was after my wife. Anybody in the company will bear me out. He wouldn't leave her alone, though she hated the sight of him, and Cap'n here give him a talking-to, didn't you, Cap? So, finally, when he wouldn't quit, then there was nothing for it but lick him. And I licked him good, and soused him in the river to get his face clean. He draws out swearing he'll get me for it. Now you know.

SHERIFF: *(To Julie)* He swears, this Pete, that you were born here in Lemoyne, and that your pop was white, and your mammy black. That right?

JULIE: That's right.

SHERIFF: *(To Parthy)* You look like a respectable woman, ma'am.

PARTHY: I am.

SHERIFF: That your little girl?

ANDY: My wife, Sheriff. And my little girl, Magnolia. What do you say to the sheriff, Magnolia?

MAGGIE: You're bad! You're a bad, mean man, that's what. You called Julie names, and made her look all funny. You're a...*(Parthy's hands stifle her)*

SHERIFF: If I was you, ma'am, I wouldn't bring no child on a boat like this. No, nor stay on it neither. Fine place to rear a child.

PARTHY: My child's as well brought up as your own—and probably better. And I'll thank you to keep your advice to yourself, Mr. Sheriff.

ANDY: Parthy! Parthy!

SHERIFF: Well, womenfolks are all alike. I'll be going. I kind of smell a nigger in the woodpile here in more ways than one. But I'll take your word for it. Only let me tell you this, Captain Hawks. You better not try to give your show in this town tonight. We got some public-spirited folks here in Lemoyne, and this fix you're in had

113

kind of leaked around. You try to give your show tonight, and first thing you know you'll be riding out of town on something don't sit so easy as a boat.

(Sheriff leaves)

ANDY: Well, Julie, my girl?
JULIE: We're going.

(On stage: Andy, Julie, and Steve)

ANDY: How're you fixed for money?
JULIE: We're fixed all right. We've been saving. You took good care of me on the "Cotton Blossom." We didn't have to spend our money.

(Steve turns to go, after shaking hands with Andy. Lights dim on cabinet Left and come up on gangplank Right as Steve and Julie leave boat. Julie looks up at the pilot house)

JULIE: I didn't say goodbye to Maggie.
ANDY: Well, you know how Parthy is, Julie. She don't mean no harm. She didn't let Maggie know what time you were going. Likely she told her it would be tomorrow. Women-folks are funny that way. She don't mean no harm.
JULIE: That's all right.

(As Julie starts across stage, Magnolia's voice is heard offstage)

MAGGIE: Let me go. Let me go. You can't keep me here. I want to see Julie.

(Parthy falls on Andy as Magnolia runs onto stage)

MAGGIE: Julie, Julie. Wait for me. I want to say goodbye. Please.

(Maggie runs across stage, then in despair, buries her face in her hands. Julie comes back on stage, and falls on her knees by Maggie and hugs her. Lights fade slightly)

PARTHY: What kind of daughter is that. Not one bit of respect for her mother.
ANDY: Good girl, Magnolia.

SCENE 3: MAGNOLIA REPLACES ELLY

(Schultzy enters, and sees a note on the table. It has his name on it. He reads it aloud, with moans.)

SCHULTZY: *(Reading)* "Dear Schultzy: Don't try to follow me, or bring me back. I'm sick of the boat, and you always telling me what to do and say. This nice man I met is going to put me as a star at the head of my own company. I intend to play Camille and, probably, Juliet. We have bookings through Illinois and Missouri, and I'm going to New York. I'm sorry to leave Cap'n Hawks in the lurch like this. I beg to remain, Yours truly, Elly Chipley or Lenore La Verne." *(He stands speechless for a moment staring)*

SCHULTZY: She can't get along without me. Juliet! Juliet! She couldn't play Little Eva without making her a slut. She's got it into her head that she's a Bernhardt, or something. Well, she'll come back. *(Andy comes in)* See this, Cap'n. *(Schultzy hands the letter to Andy)* She never packed a trunk in her life or anything. I done all those things for her. Some ways she's a child. She needed me all the time. Well, she'll come back.

ANDY: *(After reading note)* But what do we do tonight?

SCHULTZY: How about Maggie, just for tonight? She's been watching the show for a long time and should know some of it.

ANDY: Perhaps she could. We got to do something. *(Calling)* Maggie! Maggie! Come here!

(Enter Maggie and Parthy)

ANDY: Elly's left us, and we're almost sold out for tonight.

PARTHY: Fine one she is!

ANDY: Maggie, do you suppose you could say the lines well enough to get us through? Maybe Elly will come back tomorrow.

MAGNOLIA: Of course, Papa. I know every line and all the business. I'd love to do it. And I'm sure I can. *(She flings her arm around her father's neck)*

PARTHY: *(Shrieking)* Maggie! Maggie! My own daughter, an actress! That I should have lived to see this day! I'd rather have her in her grave. Why did I ever allow her to set foot on this filthy scow?

ANDY: Now, Parthy, you're just working yourself up. Matter of fact, that time Mis' Means turned her ankle, and we thought she couldn't step on it, you was all for going on in her place.

MAGNOLIA: *(Running to Parthy)* Oh, Mama. Why didn't you?

ANDY: I bet if Sophy Means hadn't tied up her foot, and gone on like the soldier she is, we'd've had you acting that night. You was raring to go. I watched you.

PARTHY: Me! Acting on the stage! Not that I couldn't play better than any Sophy Means, and that's no compliment. A poor stick if I couldn't...

ANDY: Now come on. Cheer up. Ought to be proud of your own daughter steppin' in and savin' us money. We'd've had to close.

MAGNOLIA: Mama, just for tonight? So's the show can go on.

ANDY: Now, Parthy. You can help. You give Nollie a hand with her costumes.

PARTHY: *(Almost in tears—partly pride, partly fear)* My own daughter. My little girl!

ANDY: All right. I'll give you something to screech about. We've got the biggest advance sales we've had this season. Yes, sir. Doc's raking it in with both hands. You want to have to return all that money? If you had the least bit of gumption in you, instead of screeching "My daughter, my daughter," you'd...

PARTHY: How much is the advance?

ANDY: Three hundred dollars, and it's not near opening time.

(A market woman puts her head in the door)

MARKET
WOMAN: How are you, Mis' Hawks, and Cap'n? And the little girl? My, look at the way she grown, shot up in a year's time. Well, you can't call her little girl any more. I brought you a glass of my homemade damson preserves, Mis' Hawks. I take a cup of sugar to a cup of juice. Real rich. But it is good, if I do say so myself. I told Will I was coming to the show every night you was here, and he could

like it or lump it. I been saving out of the house keeping money. This is the most exciting thing happens to us all year. Bye, now.

(Parthy has been won over)

PARTHY: Well, there's lots of sewing to be done before tonight.

MAGNOLIA: Oh, Schultzy, Let's begin. Can we get the others to rehearse now? *(Skipping around the room)* I'm going to be in the play. I'm going to be in the play tonight.

(Lights dim, then go up on boat stage where Maggie and Schultzy are rehearsing)

MAGNOLIA: Please, Schultzy. Don't throw me the line like that. I know them. I didn't stop because I was stuck.

SCHULTZY: What'd you stop for then, and look like you're scared to death?

MAGNOLIA: I stopped on purpose. She sees her husband that she hates, and has thought was dead for ten years, come sneaking in, and she wouldn't start right in to talk. She'd just stand there kind of frozen and stiff, staring at him.

SCHULTZY: *(Irritably)* All right, if you know so much about directing, go ahead and direct...

(Magnolia runs to him, and hugs him, all contrition)

MAGNOLIA: Oh, Schultzy, don't be mad. I didn't try to boss. I just wanted to act it like I felt. And I'm awfully sorry about Elly and everything. I'll do as you say, only I just can't help thinking, Schultzy dear, that she'd stand there, staring kind of silly, almost.

SCHULTZY: I guess my mind ain't on my work. I ought to know how right you are. When I got that letter Elly left for me, I just stood there gawping with my mouth open, and never said a word for I don't know how long. *(A pause)* Oh, my God.

MAGNOLIA: There, there, Schultzy.

SCHULTZY: You're right, Magnolia. That'll get them. You standing there like that, stunned and pale.

MAGNOLIA: How'll I get pale, Schultzy?

SCHULTZY: You'll feel pale inside and the audience'll think you are. Then Frank here has his sneery speech..."and so and so and so and so...and thought you'd marry the parson, huh?" And then you open up with your big scene, and so and so...

SCENE IV: THE MELODRAMA

(At the beginning of this scene a group of townspeople come down the aisles of the auditorium, talking and greeting each other. A group of musicians are leading the crowd toward the boat and on deck and continuing to play. When they are assembled and seated facing in the general direction of the stage, the house lights dim and the footlights for the show boat stage light up. As a musical introduction, a young woman sings ballads of the period accompanying herself on the guitar. The singer then becomes narrator for the play. Characters: Heroine, Fiancé, and the Villain. Narrator at stage Left)

(Heroine entering a schoolroom)

HEROINE: It brings back so many memories.

FIANCÉ: I know, dear.

HEROINE: I'm so happy now, it seems a shame to leave my schoolroom behind. But I will do anything for you—my dear.

FINANCÉ: I understand. I also have memories.

HEROINE: Oh, forgive me for being so selfish—of course you do. But this is my old schoolroom—it holds so many memories and yet everything is strange to me.

FIANCÉ: I understand.

HEROINE: Do you?

FIANCÉ: I hope with all my heart that I do.

HEROINE: Oh, you are so kind and understanding and good to me. Would it be too unkind of me to ask you to leave me alone with my schoolroom for a brief moment?

FINANCÉ: Oh, no, my dear—'tis I who was selfish—I should have known. Of course, I understand. Shall I come back later?

HEROINE: Yes, yes—I shall only be a few minutes alone. Thank you for being so understanding.

FINANCÉ: Of course—farewell, my dear. *(He leaves)*

HEROINE: Farewell. *(She waves and turns toward her room)* Farewell, dear desk. How I remember sweet Steffi Williams sitting here, with that cheery smile on her shining face, while I filled her little head with valuable knowledge. How it will help her in later life. I do miss filling those eager little minds with such knowledge. I miss it already. Ah, it seems like only yesterday. *(Touches some pencils)* Oh, and I remember when we always had a shortage of pencils. Now there are plenty, but no one to use them. And the slates which I always wrote the lessons on, and I remember when Janet had to write "I shall not pass notes in class" ten times on it. Oh, my! So many young minds have been enlightened within the small walls of this schoolroom. Sweet Nellie Olsen with her rosy dimpled cheeks sat in this room that I now say goodbye to. Farewell! Farewell, room! How I shall miss them. I am leaving one happy life to go to a happier one. I must not mourn for the joyous days gone by.

(Husband, the Villain, enters; Heroine turns, freezes, as Narrator says:)

NARRATOR: Who is this evil face confronting our lovely and trembling schoolteacher? Why, no! Horror of horrors! It couldn't be her long-lost husband who deserted her so long ago and was thought to be dead!

(Heroine screams; man in the show-boat audience shouts "Look out")

HEROINE: Oh! Who in heaven's name? Oh! *(Aside)* Could it be—he?

VILLAIN: Mind if I attend my own funeral? No—really *(laughs)* I'm alive!

HEROINE: Stay away! Everyone has said you were dead. Do not harm me, please! Stay away from me! What have you come for? What do you want of me? I'm going to be married and respectable. What do you want of me?

VILLAIN: I'm your lawful husband. Ain't I? And you've been disloyal to me.

HEROINE: But I only thought you were dead.

VILLAIN: But I ain't—see? That's your trouble. *(Laughs)* Married, huh? *(Thinks a minute, then takes it seriously)* Well, now, listen, you will not marry any vagabond bum while I'm still around!

HEROINE: He is not a vagabond...he's a preacher of the gospel and I love him. You may not sully the name of the man I love—a man of God. I love him with all my heart and soul.

VILLAIN: Ah hah! All the better. Those purified priests are all fickle on the insides.

HEROINE: No, he is not! Oh, I'm so frightened—please go away!

VILLAIN: Why should I go away? I've got no place to go and no money to go with. That's where your fickle friend comes in.

HEROINE: He hasn't any money! And I haven't any money!

VILLAIN: What about your savings?

HEROINE: I have nothing. I...OH!

(Villain grabs fair heroine and is just about to carry her away as the Fiancé steps in. A lady in the show-boat audience faints)

FIANCÉ: What is this here? Unhand her, you bumbling drunk! Who are you?

(Villain lets go heroine as she runs over and faints in hero's arms after stating faintly:)

HEROINE: He's my...husband!

VILLAIN: Yes, I'm her husband, so you have no right to her at all. *(Fiancé steps forward)* And no right to touch me. Now *(laughs)* if you will pay my way—I'll be happy to go...Uh hum—yes—now it's only a matter of money and...

(Show-boat audience hisses)

FIANCÉ: My fiancé and I owe you nothing. Now be gone before I make you gone. Do you understand?

VILLAIN: You'd better not speak to me that way—but I'll go. But I'll be back, don't you worry none! *(Exits)* I will follow you!

FIANCÉ: There now, my dear, that vulgarity has left us!

HEROINE: Oh, my lovely hero!

(Curtain falls and show-boat audience breaks into applause)

SCENE 5: IN WHICH GAYLORD RAVENAL BECOMES A MEMBER OF THE TROUPE

(Gaylord comes down the gangplank from a river boat)

POLICEMAN: Well, hello, Gaylord...you comin' back to town?

GAYLORD: As you see. What are you doing here? Waiting for me?

POLICEMAN: No. *(Pause)* No, just standing here watching the boat unload.

GAYLORD: Hmm.

POLICEMAN: How you been?

GAYLORD: Fine, thank you. Very much.

POLICEMAN: You know you gotta be outa town...this time tomorrow, don't you?

GAYLORD: I just stepped off the gangplank...that didn't take me twenty-four hours.

POLICEMAN: Yeah...yeah...well, just so's you know that's police orders for you. An' see you stay out of trouble in that twenty-four hours.

GAYLORD: Don't worry. I know.

POLICEMAN: Don't forget you gotta report to Chief of Police Vallon.

GAYLORD: *(Irritably)* Give me time, can't you?

POLICEMAN: I'm givin you time...I'm givin ya twenty-four hours.

GAYLORD: *(Pointedly)* I heard you before…Thank you!

POLICEMAN: And I know what you done before.

GAYLORD: I was acquitted, wasn't I?

POLICEMAN: Acquitted you was—but that don't change the facts none. An' what I'm sayin' is, look out about not gettin' into no more trouble.

GAYLORD: I'll look out.

(Lights dim out on them and up on the deck of the "Cotton Blossom")

PARTHY: Andy, here's a note I found. It's from Schultzy, I can hardly make it out, he writes so poorly. He's left! He's gone to find Elly. What are we goin' to do?

ANDY: *(Shaking his head)* Deserted, eh? Well, he'd be no good without Elly to fuss over, poor fool. Where's he gone?

PARTHY: Heaven knows! We don't even know where Elly is. All that big talk about going to see New York to be a big Shakespeare actress. Phooey!

ANDY: *(Scratching his whiskers)* Who've we got to play Schultzy's part?

PARTHY: Nobody…far as I can see. Oh, I wish we'd never put in to New Orleans.

DOC: *(Running in)* I heard Schultzy run away. But look, see that young man standing on the dock? He told me Schultzy was talkin' to him, about you goin' to be needin an actor. I guess somebody told Schultzy he was an actor. Better go talk to him.

PARTHY: *(Looking)* Looks kinda big for his britches—city slicker. Sort of.

ANDY: That don't mean he's a bad actor. And if we're goin' to play the bayous, we better get somebody here in the city right now. It's our only chance. We need him for now.

PARTHY: What we don't need is trouble!

ANDY: Parthy, will you quit bein' a Calamity Jane? I'm goin' down. *(Exits muttering)* Blame! Blame! Blame!

(Lights fade, then up opposite side of the stage on Ravenal)

ANDY: *(Approaching Ravenal)* I understand you've acted on the stage.

GAYLORD: I am Gaylord Ravenal of the Tennessee Ravenals…I failed to catch your name.

ANDY: *(Putting out his hand)* Andy Hawks, cap'n and owner of the Cotton Blossom floating Palace Theater.

GAYLORD: Ah, yes. *(Looks away)*

ANDY: I guess Parthy was mistaken. *(A pause)* She said that no man with cracks in his shoes would turn down…

(Gaylord looks up at the grim and ponderous figure on the forward deck of the show boat)

GAYLORD: That…the…lady…

ANDY: My wife…We've lost our juvenile lead…Fifteen a week and found…It's a chance…a chance to see the world…No responsibility…I said…uh…Parthy said…

GAYLORD: Am I to understand that I'm being…uh…offered the position of juvenile lead on the…ah…Cotton Blossom Floating Palace?

ANDY: That's the size of it. No responsibility. *(Gaylord laughs)* A chance to see life!

GAYLORD: I've seen it.

ANDY: We do some mighty fine work…fresh from New York.

GAYLORD: Hmm.

120

(Magnolia appears on deck ready to go into town)

GAYLORD: Is that a member of your company?

ANDY: That...that's my daughter, Magnolia.

GAYLORD: Magnolia...Magnol...Does she...is she an...

ANDY: I should smile she is. She's our ingenue lead...Magnolia. Plays opposite the juvenile lead, but if you've been a trouper you know that I guess. Say, young man, what's your name? Oh yes, Ravenal...Well, Ravenal, you a quick study? That's what I have to know first off, because we leave New Orleans tonight to play the bayous. Bayou Teche tomorrow night to play "In Tempest and Sunshine." You a quick study?

(During all of the above speech Gaylord has been gazing at Magnolia without taking his eyes off her)

GAYLORD: Lightning.

ANDY: Well now, young man, I aim to give you a try. You sure you can get up in the part by tomorrow night?

GAYLORD: Absolutely certain. *(Still gazing)*

ANDY: Then I'm goin' to take you up on deck, to meet Mrs. Hawks and Magnolia...Mind you, I'm the boss here, but I like Parthy and Magnolia to kinda know what's goin' on.

(They go up the gangplank and in pantomime Gaylord meets Parthy and Maggie. Gaylord starts talking to Maggie as Parthy pulls Andy aside. Lights up on opposite side of stage)

PARTHY: *(To Andy)* I tell you I can't bear the sight of him! Palaverin' and soft-soaping. Bending over my hand like I was sort of a princess or somethin'. Thinks he can get around me that way, does he? Well, I'll bet I'm worth a dozen of him when it comes to being smart...even if I don't go around kissing total strangers.

ANDY: Yes, I know that. But you're not about to play the juvenile lead, smart or not.

PARTHY: He LOOKS at Magnolia, I tell you.

ANDY: Fool if he didn't.

PARTHY: Andy Hawks, you mean to stand there and tell me you'd as lief see your daughter takin' up with a wharf rat...or worse.

ANDY: Ooooooooooohhhhhh. *(In pain at her bickering)*

PARTHY: Well, I aim to find out.

SCENE 6: OUT RIDING WITH A MURDERER

(Parthy comes striding down the aisle of the auditorium as if from town, Frank struggling to keep up with her)

PARTHY: Andy, Andy Hawks. Do you know where your daughter is?

FRANK: Hold on...not so fast!

PARTHY: I saw them! Together on Canal Street! Riding in...in a carriage...*(choked)* with a murderer!

ANDY: What? What's the matter, woman? Huh? Tell me what's the matter, what's goin' on?

PARTHY: He's a murderer...He said so...the Chief of Police said so.

ANDY: Who's a murderer...the Chief of Police?

PARTHY: No! Rav—(Chokes with rage again)

ANDY: Tell me what this is, Frank.

FRANK: Ravenal's a murderer, and him and your daughter were riding in a carriage.

PARTHY: With a murderer. Together. Ravenal killed a man!

ANDY: (To Frank) Why didn't you chase him?

FRANK: (Pointing to Parthy) I was chasing her.

ANDY: Well, who did he murder?

PARTHY: How am I supposed to know?

ANDY: If he is a murderer why wasn't he hanged?

FRANK: He was acquitted. Said it was self-defense.

ANDY: If he was acquitted then he can't be that bad.

PARTHY: Any murderer is dangerous and your daughter is riding with one. What are you going to do about it?

ANDY: Do about it? What is there to do? Oh, murderers be damned! I killed a man when I was nineteen, Mrs. Hawks, and been twenty-five years a respected man. And that's the truth if you want to talk about murderers!

(Parthy faints)

SCENE 7: IN WHICH MAGNOLIA LEAVES THE COTTON BLOSSOM

(Parthy in widow's weeds. Magnolia enters)

MAGNOLIA: Now that Papa is gone, you'll probably want to stay in Thebes, summer as well as winter.

PARTHY: Thebes! I'll do nothing of the kind, miss! If you and that fine husband of yours think to rid yourself of me that way...

MAGNOLIA: But, Mama, we're not trying to rid ourselves of you. How can you think of such things? You've always said you hated the boat. And now that Papa...now that you needn't stay with the show any longer, I thought you'd want to go back to Thebes to live.

PARTHY: Indeed? And what's to become of the "Cotton Blossom," tell me that, Maggie Hawks?

MAGNOLIA: I don't know. I don't know. That's what I think we ought to talk about.

(Windy comes in and listens)

PARTHY: Well, we're talking about it, ain't we? Your Pa left no will. Just like him! I've as much say-so as you have. More. I'm his widow. You won't see me willing to throw away the goodwill of a business that it's taken years to build up. The boat's insurance'll take care of the repairs. Your Pa's life insurance is paid up, and quite a decent sum. You'll get your share; I'll get mine. The boat goes on as it always has. No Thebes for me. You'll go on playing ingenue leads; Ravenal will play juvenile.

MAGNOLIA: I must talk with Gay about this.

PARTHY: (As Magnolia leaves) Oh, I'm sure you must.

WINDY: Mis' Hawks. You're Hawks' widow. That's why I said I'd take her same's if Andy was alive. I thought Magnolia's husband would boss this boat, but seems you're running it. Well, ma'am. I ain't no petticoat pilot. I'm off the end of this trip down. Young Tanner'll come aboard there and pilot you.

PARTHY: Tanner! Who's he? How do you know I want him? I'm running this boat.

WINDY: You better take him, Mis' Hawks, ma'am. He's young and not set in his ways, and likely won't mind your nagging. I'm too old. Well, ma'am, I'm going.

(He comes to her and shakes hands, then leaves. Magnolia returns)

MAGNOLIA: Gay says it won't work. He thinks we should leave the boat.

PARTHY: Where you going with that fine husband of yours? Tell me that.

MAGNOLIA: I don't know.

PARTHY: I'll warrant you don't. No more does he. Why're you going? You've got a good home on the boat.

MAGNOLIA: We're not...I'm not...Well, Gay's not happy any more on the river.

PARTHY: You'll be a sight unhappier on land before you're through. Make no mistake about that, young lady. Where'll you go? Chicago, hmm? What'll you do there? Starve and worse, I know. Many's the time you'll wish yourself back here.

MAGNOLIA: *(Almost shouting)* How do you know? How can you be so sure? And even if you are right, what of it? You're always trying to keep people from doing the things they want to do. You fought to keep Papa from buying the "Cotton Blossom" in the first place. And now you won't leave it. You didn't want me to act. You didn't want me to marry Gay. You didn't want me to have Kim. Maybe you were right. Maybe I shouldn't have done any of those things. But how do you know that even when you're right, you mayn't be wrong? If Papa had listened to you, we'd be living in Thebes. He'd be alive, probably, I'd be married to the butcher, maybe. You can't do it. Even God lets people have their own way, though they have to fall down and break their necks to find they were wrong. But you seem glad when it turns out badly.

PARTHY: That's enough of that, Maggie. We must talk of dividing up the money. Why don't you retain your share in the boat, and I'll send you your share of the profits at regular intervals?

MAGNOLIA: No, we'd rather sell our share outright to you. I think Gay wants to invest it in a business on land.

PARTHY: Monkey business, probably. Mark my words, I don't say I wouldn't be glad to see you and Kim back. But not him. When he's run through every penny, he needn't look to me for more. I'm through with him.

MAGNOLIA: Then you're through with me, too. For I am leaving with my husband.

PARTHY: Well, the show boat is going on!

(Parthy stands alone on the stage shouting after Magnolia and Ravenal as they go up the aisle of the auditorium and out. The lights dim as she stands there)

END

Suggested Novels & Reference Books

Remember when you read a novel that you cannot hope to dramatize every event. You select those episodes that move the plot forward and fit in with the theme that you and children choose. Even though a book may have many episodes that are not stageable, such as battles, ocean voyages, long treks across a plain, if it still has enough personal relationships and indoor scenes, it can be made into a dramatic production. Traditional ways of handling unstageable scenes are by having a narrator or a speaking chorus. However, you can just eliminate them, and let their effect be made evident. For example, in *1776* a messenger comes *from* General Washington, and we do not have to *see* the general or his troops.

Don't forget that you should ask the publisher's permission before dramatizing a copyrighted book.

HISTORICAL NOVELS

Shakespeare's England

Bennett, John. *Master Skylark*. Grosset, 1924.
   (A boy in England in Shakespeare's time.)
Chute, Marchette. *The Wonderful Winter*. Dutton, 1954.
   (A boy in England in Shakespeare's time.)
DeAngeli, Marguerite. *The Door in the Wall*. Doubleday, 1949.
   (A crippled boy during the great plague in London in 1665.)
Gray, Elizabeth Janet. *Adam of the Road*. Viking, 1942.
   (Adventures of a boy in England in Shakespeare's time.)
Gray, Elizabeth Janet. *I Will Adventure*. Viking, 1962.
   (A twelve-year-old boy in England, fascinated by the theater, meets Shakespeare.)

Norsemen in America

Coatsworth, Elizabeth. *Door to the North*. Holt, Rinehart and Winston, 1950.
   ("A Saga of 14th Century America"—adventures of the Norsemen, based on authoritative theories of their settlements.)

North American Indians

Farnsworth, Frances Joyce. *Winged Moccasins*. Messner, 1954.
   (The story of Sacajawea, who helped Lewis and Clark.)
Haller, Adolf. *He Served Two Masters*. Pantheon, 1962.
   (A boy serving under Cortes in Mexico in 1519.)
Montgomery, Jean. *The Wrath of Coyote*. Morrow, 1968.
   (Indian side of the story of the Spanish conquest.)

South American Indians

Clark, Ann Nolan. *Secret of the Andes*. Viking, 1952.
   (A modern Inca boy herds llamas in a beautiful valley in the mountains of Peru.)

Colonial America

Berry, Erick. *Seven Beaver Skins.* Winston, 1948.
(A story of the Dutch in New Amsterdam. Out of print, but in some libraries.)
Coatsworth, Elizabeth. *The Last Fort.* Holt, Rinehart, 1952.
(A story of the French voyageurs just after the French and Indian War in 1763.)
Eaton, Jeanette. *Lone Journey.* Harcourt, Brace, 1944.
(Roger Williams and the founding of Rhode Island.)
Faulkner, Nancy. *A Stage for Rom.* E. M. Hale & Co., 1962.
(A boy and his sister in Williamsburg, Virginia, in colonial days.)
Field, Rachel. *Calico Bush.* Macmillan, 1966.
(A "bound-out" girl in Maine in 1743.)
Graham, Shirley. *The Story of Phillis Wheatley.* Messner, 1949.
(A little slave girl in Boston who became a famous poet.)
Gray, Elizabeth Janet. *Meggy MacIntosh.* Viking, 1930.
(A Scottish girl coming to America in colonial times.)
Long, L. *John Peter Zenger.* Bobbs Merrill, 1966.
(The man who fought for freedom of the press in New York City in colonial times.)
Petry, Ann. *Tibuba of Salem Village.* Crowell, 1964.
(A very intelligent slave from Jamaica and her husband become victimized by the religious hysteria at the time of the witch trials in Salem.)
Speare, Elizabeth George. *Calico Captive.* Houghton Mifflin, 1957.
(A young woman in New Hampshire and in Canada during the French and Indian War.)
Speare, Elizabeth George. *Witch of Blackbird Pond.* Houghton Mifflin, 1958.
(A young woman falsely accused of being a witch in colonial Connecticut.)

American Revolution

Brown, S. *Ethan Allen and the Green Mountain Boys.* Random, 1956.
(Colonial quarrels between Vermont and New York.)
Fast, Howard. *Haym Solomon.* Messner, 1941.
(A man who aided George Washington financially during the Revolutionary War. He lived in New York and Philadelphia.)
Forbes, Esther. *Johnny Tremain.* Houghton Mifflin, 1943. Paperback, Dell, 1968.
(A boy in Boston during the Revolutionary period.)
Fritz, Jean. *Early Thunder.* Coward McCann, 1967.
(A boy's adventures during the American Revolution.)
Sperry, Armstrong. *John Paul Jones, Fighting Sailor.* Random, 1953.
Stevenson, A. *Paul Revere, Boy of Old Boston.* Bobbs-Merrill, 1946.
(American Revolution story.)
Wibberley, Leonard. *Young Man from the Piedmont.* Farrar, Strauss, 1963.
(The young Thomas Jefferson.)

Pre-Civil War

Benet, Stephen Vincent. *The Devil and Daniel Webster.* Holt, Rinehart & Winston, 1937.
(The setting is New Hampshire about 1850.)

Civil War

Alcott, Louisa. *Little Women.* Little, Brown, 1968 (and many other editions).
(Good play for girls.)
Fritz, Jean. *Brady.* Coward McCann, 1960.
(A story of the underground railroad, and a young boy in Civil War days.)
Hunt, Irene. *Across Five Aprils.* Follett, 1964.
(A boy of ten years in Illinois during the Civil War.)
Levy, Mimi. *Corrie and the Yankee.* Viking, 1959.
(A girl in the South during the Civil War.)
West, Jessamyn. *The Friendly Persuasion.* Harcourt, 1956; also available in paperback.
(Charming story of a Quaker family in Ohio in Civil War times.)

Slavery and afterward

Bernard, Jacqueline. *Journey Toward Freedom*. W. W. Norton, 1967. Paperback, Dell, 1969.
("The Story of Sojourner Truth.")

Benet, Stephen Vincent. *John Brown's Body*. Holt, Rinehart & Winston, 1941.
(A book-length poem dealing with the South, slavery, and the uprising at Harper's Ferry.)

Bontemps, Arno. *Chariot in the Sky*. Holt, Rinehart & Winston, 1951.
(A story of the Jubilee Singers of Fisk University about 1873.)

Douglass, Frederick. *The Life and Times of Frederick Douglass*, adapted by Barbara Ritchie.
Thomas Y. Crowell, 1966.

Petry, Ann. *Harriet Tubman*. Thomas Y. Crowell, 1955.
(A conductor on the underground railroad. This is very dramatic, but all the trips of the underground railroad must either be stylized, or two or three episodes extracted from all the trips.)

Sterling, Dorothy. *Captain of the Planter*. Doubleday, 1958.
(The true story of Robert Small, a slave who became free.)

Sterne, Emma Gelders. *The Long Black Schooner*. Follett, 1968.
(The voyage of the *Amistad,* based on newspaper accounts and court records. It is about kidnapped Africans in 1830, destined for slavery.)

Yates, Elizabeth. *Amos Fortune, Free Man*. Dutton, 1950.
(A Negro slave who earned his freedom in New Hampshire.)

The West

Baker, Betty. *Walk the World's Rim*. Harper & Row, 1965.
(A boy traveling with the Spaniards from Texas to Mexico City in the sixteenth century.)

Johnson, Annabel and Edgar. *Torrie*. Harper, 1960.
(A fourteen-year-old girl traveling in a covered wagon in 1846 from St. Louis to California.)

Lane, Rose Wilder. *Let the Hurricane Roar*. McKay, 1933.
(A vivid story of settling in the West, but there are only a few characters involved.)

Meader, Stephen W. *Jonathan Goes West*. Harcourt, Brace, 1946.
(Story of a boy traveling from Maine to Illinois by many different conveyances in 1845.)

Morrow, Honore. *On to Oregon*. Morrow, 1926.
(Story of the Sager family in 1844. They left home in Missouri to make the 2,000-mile journey to Oregon by covered wagon in 1844.)

REFERENCE BOOKS

Arbuthnot, May, et al. *Children's Books Too Good to Miss,* 6th edn. Press of Case Western Reserve University, 1966.

Arno Press. *Complete Catalog of Books 1970/71.* Arno Press, 330 Madison Avenue, New York.
(An excellent collection of original sources arranged in an annotated list that would be useful to every history teacher.)

Barnes, Douglas. *Drama in the English Classroom*. National Council of Teachers of English, 508 S. Sixth St., Champaign, Ill., 1968. (A pamphlet that includes a section, "Initiating the Use of Drama," that will be particularly helpful to the non-theater-trained classroom teacher. The pamphlet is about a 1966 Dartmouth seminar on teaching English.)

Butterfield, Roger. *The American Past,* 2d rev. ed. Simon and Schuster, 1966. (The illustrations are particularly helpful.)

Harris, Peter, ed. *Drama in Education,* vol. 3 of *English in Education.* The Bodley Head, London, 1967. (A pamphlet with interesting essays about drama in school situations in England.)

The Horn Book Magazine. Horn Book Inc., 585 Boylston St., Boston, Mass. (Excellent reviews of new and old books for children.)

Huberman, Leo. *We the People*. Monthly Review, 1964.

McCalmon, George, and Christian Moe. *Creating Historical Drama*. Southern Illinois University Press. (Although this is not intended for schools, it is an excellent account of creating historical drama in various communities.)

McCaslin, Nellie. *Creative Dramatics in the Classroom*. McKay, 1968. (A scholarly presentation for teachers of the possibilities of using dramatics in classrooms, especially in elementary schools. There is a helpful bibliography.)

Mackenzie, David, and William B. Blankenburg. *Never Give a Lady a Restive Horse*. Paperback, Diablo Press, 1967. (About etiquette.)

Oxenford, Lyn. *Playing Period Plays*. Coach House Press.

Tunis, Edwin. *Colonial Living*. World, 1957. (Beautiful drawings and excellent descriptions.)

Twain, Mark. *Life on the Mississippi*. Dodd, Mead (and many other editions).

Ward, Winifred. *Playmaking with Children*, 2nd edn. Appleton-Century-Crofts, 1957. (Miss Ward's inimitable account of how to go about improvising on a story or an idea with children, to make a play and a full production. A real help to anyone planning to work this way.)

  Stories to Dramatize. Anchorage Press, 1952. (A selection of poems and plays for dramatization. No historical novels such as we have used, but a good selection for younger children.)

  Theatre for Children, rev. edn. Appleton-Century-Croft, 1958. (One of the oldest and best of the books on children's theater. It includes both history and present-day playmaking.)

References for music

Boni, Margaret Bradford, ed. *The Fireside Book of Favorite American Songs*. Simon and Schuster, 1952.

Lomax, Alan. *The Folk Songs of North America*. Doubleday, 1960.

Index